AVOIDING THE FALL

CARNEGIE
ENDOWMENT FOR
INTERNATIONAL PEACE

MICHAEL ★ PETTIS

AVOIDING
THE
FALL

CHINA'S ECONOMIC
RESTRUCTURING

Carnegie Endowment for International Peace
1779 Massachusetts Avenue, N.W., Washington, D.C. 20036
202-483-7600, Fax 202-483-1840
www.ceip.org

The Carnegie Endowment does not take institutional positions on public policy issues; the views represented herein are the author's own and do not necessarily reflect the views of Carnegie, its staff, or its trustees.

To order, contact:
Hopkins Fulfillment Service
P.O. Box 50370, Baltimore, MD 21211-4370
1-800-537-5487 or 1-410-516-6956
Fax 1-410-516-6998

Library of Congress Cataloging-in-Publication Data
Pettis, Michael.
Avoiding the fall : China's economic restructuring / Michael Pettis.
pages cm.
Includes bibliographical references and index.
ISBN 978-0-87003-407-7 (pbk.) – ISBN 978-0-87003-406-0 (cloth)
– ISBN 978-0-87003-408-4 (electronic)
1. China–Economic policy–2000- 2. China–Economic conditions–2000-
I. Carnegie Endowment for International Peace. II. Title.

HC427.95.P48 2013
330.951 – dc23

MIX
Paper from
responsible sources
FSC
www.fsc.org
FSC® C010236

CONTENTS

FOREWORD

Some experts and markets continue to be bullish about the Chinese economy, expecting that high rates of growth will continue indefinitely. But that focus on numbers obscures stark realities.

While the country certainly achieved remarkable growth over the last three decades, success came with significant costs. Like other rapidly developing Asian economies, China relied on repressed household consumption to make modernizing investments. Its economic model distorted interest rates, the currency, and even legal structures. And it led to burgeoning debt that is becoming increasingly difficult to finance. The time has come for China to adjust its model to the new circumstances success has produced.

Significant challenges lie ahead. To sustain growth, employment, and social stability, China must now deal with lagging wage growth, financial repression, environmental degradation, and the development of a social safety net.

In *Avoiding the Fall*, Michael Pettis offers a fresh look at China's economic situation and upends much conventional wisdom. A professor of finance at Peking University's Guanghua School of Management with extensive Wall Street experience and an intimate knowledge of China, Pettis offers unique insight.

In his cogent analysis of the Chinese economy, Pettis exposes the flaws in many analyses that often rely solely on past performance. And he assesses the potential impact of the six options China has for restructuring its economy.

It is clear that China needs to reform its development model to achieve a very different kind of growth. Rebalancing is inevitable, but the question is how it will occur. Whatever Beijing decides will have huge implications for the global economy.

Pettis wisely challenges the widely held myth that China's rise will continue without reform. This book is essential reading for anyone looking to better understand the world's second-largest economy and the difficult economic changes that lie ahead.

DOUGLAS H. PAAL
Vice President for Studies
Carnegie Endowment for International Peace

CHAPTER 1

THE LIMITS OF THE CHINESE GROWTH MODEL

Beijing began to reform the Chinese economy in the late 1970s and early 1980s. Since then it managed to generate such spectacular growth for three decades that, with the possible exception of postwar Japan, South Korea, and Taiwan, no comparable precedents exist. Even these limited precedents may understate China's achievement.

Japan's success occurred in a country that had been economically destroyed by war but that had been socially and culturally an advanced economy since at least the end of the nineteenth century. It was already the sixth-largest manufacturing nation by the 1920s, surpassed only by the United States, Germany, Britain, France, and the USSR.[1] As the cases of Germany after 1945 and Belgium after 1918 suggest, advanced countries destroyed by war tend to catch up to their former status very quickly, perhaps because they start the process with much higher levels of social capital and institutional frameworks that permit and encourage rapid growth in productivity.

For this reason, in some ways Taiwan and South Korea may be more useful comparisons to China. They are among the very few economies in the twentieth century to have transformed from poor-country status to rich-country status. Indeed, South Korea began its process of dramatic growth much more socially and economically backward than China was at a comparable time in its development. Still, South Korea and Taiwan

---

1   Michael Lind, *Land of Promise: An Economic History of the United States* (New York: HarperCollins, 2012), 263.

both benefited from their strategic roles in the Cold War, when the United States and its allies considered it vitally important that they emerge as great economic successes.

China, of course, had no equivalent backing, and if today it is still much poorer than South Korea and Taiwan, its tremendous growth over the past three decades is in many ways comparable to their achievement. Granted, much of China's growth, especially during the first decade of the reform period, came about largely as a function of Beijing's reversal of constraining policies put into place during the Maoist period. In the late 1970s, for example, China had fallen far behind neighboring countries that had been at similar or much lower levels of economic development in the 1920s and 1930s. Simply by eliminating the constraints imposed as a consequence of these policies, Beijing allowed China sufficient leeway to catch up to where it might have otherwise been under conditions more favorable to normal economic growth.[2]

But just reversing bad policies is not enough to explain all that has occurred in the past three decades. Beijing has learned well from the history of other developing countries, and it has applied some of those lessons carefully and intelligently. Taking its cues from other countries that had experienced rapid growth, especially Asian countries that followed the growth model that Japan had partly put into place in the late nineteenth and early twentieth centuries, and which it had renewed in the postwar period, China was able to push much further than it otherwise would have. During this period China joined a group of countries whose growth rates were so high during one or more decades of the twentieth century that they were characterized as economic "miracles."

But there's the rub. With the exception of South Korea, Taiwan, and perhaps Chile, none of the many "miracle" economies of the twentieth century has been able to sustain growth to the point where it was able to join the rich-country club, and Japan had already been a member of the club when its growth miracle began. In the late 1980s, University of Chicago Professor Robert Aliber proposed, partly in jest, what he called the

---

2 Barry Naughton, *Growing Out of the Plan: Chinese Economic Reform, 1978–1993* (Cambridge: Cambridge University Press, 1996).

Andy Warhol theory of economic growth: "In the future every country will grow rapidly for fifteen years."

But, as he notes, this growth isn't enough to ensure continued success. In every case, I will argue in this book, decades of high growth, almost always driven by very high levels of investment, eventually faltered. Even among the "successful" countries, the period of growth was interrupted in every case either by a debt crisis and many years of negative growth or by a lost decade of very slow growth and burgeoning debt.

So why were a few countries able to overcome the interruption in growth while most were not? The most obvious answer, and perhaps nearly a truism, is that the successful countries made the necessary reforms before and during the various crisis periods—and there were always more than one—that allowed them to rebalance and restructure their economies in ways that permitted further growth. In other countries, the less successful ones, domestic distortions, often political in nature, prevented the kinds of economic changes that were necessary to permit the country to keep growing in a healthy way.[3]

China today is facing a similar challenge. For much of the past decade, a few economists had argued that distortions and imbalances in China's growth model had become so severe that, unless they were corrected, China's growth miracle would soon come to an end and would be difficult to revive. Rapid growth in China had come at the expense of significant distortions in interest rates, wages, currency, and legal structures, along with political capture of the benefits of growth. One of the results—a nearly inevitable result, as I will show—was a very distorted national balance sheet with burgeoning debt and decreasing ability to finance that debt.

This argument has not always been popular, especially among Chinese and foreign commentators most captivated by the story of China's inevitable rise. But it is nonetheless now clear that China must come to terms with these distortions and reverse them, and that this will prove difficult.

---

3 See Ricardo Ffrench-Davies, ed., *Financial Crises in "Successful" Emerging Economies* (Washington, D.C.: Brookings Institution Press, 2001), and Jeffry A. Frieden, *Debt, Development and Democracy: Modern Political Economy and Latin America 1965–1985* (Princeton, N.J.: Princeton University Press, 1992).

Although for many years the China skeptics were very much in a minority amid the sometimes gushing and largely ahistorical analysis provided by most experts and commentators on China, by early 2012 it had become increasingly obvious to most economists that the development model that had generated spectacular growth for the Chinese economy over the past three decades had reached its limits.

More worryingly, the distortions that accompanied the furious growth, especially distortions in the financial sector, were becoming increasingly difficult to resolve even as the costs they imposed on the economy rose. "If something cannot go on forever, it will stop," Herb Stein, President Richard Nixon's economic adviser, famously pointed out in the 1980s. He was discussing current account deficits, but it has been only in the past two to three years that the consensus among economists has recognized that this simple and obvious dictum applies also to China.

China, in other words, has no choice but to rebalance and restructure its economy. With China's most recent change in Communist Party leadership taking place in October 2012, followed by corresponding changes in the national leadership in March 2013, there is widespread agreement among analysts that Beijing must put into place measures that unwind the distortions and eliminate the domestic imbalances. Even many of those who as recently as two to three years ago argued that the underlying growth model was serving China well now agree on the need to rebalance and restructure.

If it fails to act, China probably faces the kind of crisis suffered by nearly every other country that has followed a similar investment-driven growth model. There is a great deal of discussion over what the corrective measures should be, with many of them focusing on Beijing's stated intentions and on the political limitations imposed by the country's governance system.

It seems that nearly everyone from the former premier, Wen Jiabao, and the current premier, Li Keqiang, on down has come to agree that Beijing's consumption imbalance has reached dangerous levels and that China must rebalance. Here, for example, is the *South China Morning Post* on the subject in early 2012:

"China is landing quite well. Its inflation is down, investment and growth has slowed," said Zhu Min, IMF deputy managing director, yesterday during his first speech in Hong Kong since assuming his new position in July of last year. "However, it still needs to carefully manage its investment-driven development model, as investment takes up about 48 per cent of gross domestic product."

Zhu's words echoed a string of heavyweight calls for reform, including ones from Premier Wen Jiabao and Vice-Premier Li Keqiang and scholars at China's central bank and the national state council. Li said over the weekend that "reforms have entered a tough stage," and that "China has reached a crucial period in changing its economic model and [change] cannot be delayed."

The fear is that the current situation, in which exports and investment contribute to most of China's GDP growth, is no longer sustainable. Export growth to Europe, the largest trading partner with China, had dropped almost to zero, and an investment driven economy had left the country with a huge pile of debt that could potentially go sour, economists said.[4]

THE CHONGQING MODEL—CHINA WRIT SMALL

The sudden but not wholly unexpected removal of Bo Xilai as party secretary of Chongqing in March 2012 only intensified the debate over the nature of the reforms. Bo Xilai was a rising populist figure within the country's elite whose management of Chongqing, a municipality in central China with a population of over thirty million, had created what was widely referred to as the "Chongqing" model of economic development. This model consists largely of an extension and intensification of the growth model in place in China over the past decade, but with greater emphasis on state control and income redistribution.

In opposition to the Chongqing model is the "Guangdong" model, which emphasizes governance reform, banking liberalization, and a strengthening of the role of the private sector. The Guangdong model

---

4 Lulu Chen, "IMF Predicts Soft Landing ... With Advice for Beijing," *South China Morning Post*, March 20, 2012.

and other reform models share a concern over the long-term economic costs associated with the maintenance of China's existing growth model.

After the initial shock associated with Bo Xilai's removal wore off, much of the speculation within China moved on to what his ouster said about the evolution of power within China and, for economists, how it would affect the reform and rebalancing of the Chinese economy. In this book I won't have a whole lot to say about the politics of the leadership transition, in no small part because, frankly, other than the members of the Standing Committee, the Politburo, the State Council, and a few other very plugged-in individuals, few of us can say anything about the implications of the Bo Xilai scandal that isn't largely speculative.

More importantly, I believe that when projecting China's future, too many analysts may have systematically overemphasized the intentions of the Chinese leadership. If Beijing announces that it plans to accomplish a specific goal—raise the consumption share of GDP, for example, or double the length of railroad track, or double household income in ten years—analysts quickly incorporate that goal into their projections even when it isn't at all clear how Beijing will accomplish it.

This failure to focus on constraints is one of the important reasons that I think most analysts have gotten China fundamentally wrong in the past five to ten years. By misunderstanding how China's growth model works, and how the functioning of the model forces certain kinds of behavior and prevents other kinds of behavior, they have been much less skeptical about Beijing's ability to execute its intentions than perhaps they should have been. Any economic model creates its own constraints. In the short term, leaders can engage in policies that temporarily seem to violate these economic constraints, but the longer this goes on, the more difficult those constraints become, until eventually the policies reach their limits.

While intentions matter in the short term, in other words, over the medium and long term we should be much less impressed by what the leaders say they will do and much more concerned about how the constraints they face will limit what they actually can do. As I will show later in the book, much of what Beijing has done in the past few years was possible only because it had significant debt capacity: it was able to raise debt quickly in order to generate waves of investment that allowed Beijing to avoid the constraints created by its development model.

But each time it did so, its ability to raise debt further was constrained, because debt rose faster than the means by which the debt was to be serviced. For this reason, Beijing's earlier "successes" in violating economic constraints should in no way imply that it can continue to be successful in the same way going forward.

This is an issue not just for China, by the way, but for any country. For example, knowing the constraints imposed on Europe by the functioning of the balance of payments, we should be wholly unimpressed by what many senior German and European leaders say they expect to happen to resolve Europe's debt crisis. The fact is that if we hope to see net repayments by peripheral Europe to Germany, we will also have to see a reversal in their respective current account positions. Spain cannot repay its debt, in other words, and Germany cannot stop exporting capital (mainly to peripheral Europe), until Spain runs a current account surplus and Germany a current account deficit.

Any plan to resolve the European crisis is useless unless it specifies the conditions under which this reversal of the respective current accounts will take place. So far neither of these scenarios seems likely. But without a reversal of the current account positions, in which Spain is able to repay its debt to Germany, is not just unlikely but impossible, no matter how determined Madrid, Rome, Berlin, and Paris might be to reduce debt in an orderly way.

The case of Europe is instructive for a couple of reasons. First, the continuing European crisis will make China's own adjustment over the next few years both far more urgent and far more difficult. Second, it shows that the need to meet accounting identities and the associated economic constraints applies to every country, including China. No matter how sincere its intentions, what Beijing says it will do over the next few years is meaningful only if its policies are internally consistent and do not violate accounting constraints.

In this book I will describe China's growth model, discuss how it reached the current level of domestic imbalance, and lay out as logically as possible the economic options available to Beijing in order for China to rebalance its economy, with some discussion of the limitations of each of these options. Any decision made by Beijing that is not consistent with these options, I will argue, should not be taken seriously as a prediction of the future because it is almost by definition unsustainable.

China has no choice but to rebalance its economy; the only question is the manner in which it does so. Rebalancing will happen either in a less painful and more orderly way, as a consequence of specific steps enacted by Beijing, or in a more painful and disorderly way, as a consequence of the imposition of constraints. But either way, it will happen.

WHAT IS REBALANCING?

To try to work out what these options might be, I will begin with two key assumptions. The first is that the fundamental imbalance in China is the very low GDP share of consumption. This low GDP share, I will argue, reflects a growth model that systematically forces up the savings rate largely by repressing consumption growth. It does this by effectively transferring wealth from the household sector (in the form, among others, of very low interest rates, an undervalued currency, and relatively slow wage growth) in order to subsidize and generate rapid GDP growth. All of this will be explained in more detail in chapter 2.

As a consequence of this consumption-repressing growth model, Chinese growth is driven largely by the need to keep investment levels extraordinarily high. What's more, the very high growth rate in investment, combined with significant pricing distortions, especially in the cost of capital, has resulted in overinvestment, which in turn has led to an unsustainable increase in debt. China cannot slow the growth in debt and resolve its internal economic problems without raising the consumption share of GDP.[5]

My second major assumption is that China must and will rebalance in the coming years—its imbalances cannot get much greater, nor can they be sustained at these levels. We must soon see, therefore, a reversal of these imbalances either because Beijing chooses to reverse the imbalances or because the accompanying constraints will force a rebalancing onto the economy.

---

5   This is not a recent problem. See Nicholas Lardy, *China's Unfinished Economic Revolution* (Washington, D.C.: Brookings Institution Press, 1998).

There are two reasons for saying that, one way or the other, China will rebalance in the coming years, neither of which has to do with the claims being made by Beijing that China is indeed determined to rebalance its economy. The first reason is a function of the country's debt dynamics. Every country that has followed a consumption-repressing, investment-driven growth model like China's has ended with an unsustainable debt burden caused by wasted debt-financed investment. This has always led to either a debt crisis or a lost decade of very low growth.

At some point the debt burden itself poses a limit to the continuation of the growth model and forces rebalancing toward a higher consumption share of GDP. The reason for this has to do with limits to an increase in debt. As I will discuss later in this book, when debt capacity limits are reached, investment must drop because it can no longer be funded quickly enough to generate growth. As this occurs, China will automatically rebalance, but it will rebalance through a collapse in GDP growth that might even go negative, resulting in a rising share of consumption only because consumption does not drop as quickly as GDP. As I will show, this is what happened in the United States in the early 1930s.

I must stress that I am not saying that a collapse in the Chinese economy is inevitable. My argument here is only that if the unsustainable rise in debt isn't addressed and reversed in a way that rebalances the economy gradually, China, or any other country for that matter, would eventually reach its debt capacity limit, and that in turn would force a catastrophic rebalancing of its economy away from investment.

The good news, however, is that because there is a growing awareness of the costs of the imbalances and the risk of a debt crisis, Beijing will probably begin rebalancing before it reaches the debt capacity limit. I will discuss later how Beijing can engineer the rebalancing process, but the point here is just that either Beijing forces rebalancing, or rebalancing will be forced upon China in the form of a debt crisis. Whichever way prevails, in other words, debt will force China to rebalance.

The second reason for assuming that China will rebalance is because of external constraints. Globally, savings and investment must balance. This means that for any set of countries whose savings exceed investment, like China, there must be countries whose investment exceeds savings, like the United States. To put it another way, the world can function with a group of underconsuming countries only if they are balanced by a group of overconsuming countries.

For the past decade the underconsuming countries of central Europe and Asia, of which China was by far the most important, were balanced by overconsuming countries in peripheral Europe and North America. Globally the total amount of savings is equal to the total amount of investment, and so if some countries forced up their savings rates faster than their increase in investment, this had to be matched by a group of countries whose savings rates dropped relative to investment. This, of course, is an accounting identity whose constraints cannot be breached.

But conditions are changing. The overconsuming countries of North America and peripheral Europe are being forced to reduce their overconsumption (in the latter case) or are working toward reducing it (in the former case). To the extent they succeed, by definition unless there is a surge in global investment—which given the weak state of the world is very unlikely—underconsuming countries must increase their total consumption rates, or else the world economy cannot balance savings and investment except through negative growth.

This may sound surprising, but it follows automatically from the accounting identities. Because investment and savings must balance, if a reduction in consumption in the overconsuming countries is not met by an equal increase in consumption in the under-consuming countries, then by definition for any given level of GDP the savings rate will tend to be forced up.

If investment doesn't rise, however, then savings cannot rise either (the two must balance), and so some mechanism will prevent the savings rate from rising. This mechanism will be a contraction in GDP. Lower consumption that is not matched by higher investment means, by definition, that global demand will contract, and as global demand contracts, global production must contract, too, in order to meet that demand.

This is just another way of saying that global GDP growth must become negative. And as GDP growth goes negative, the difference between GDP and consumption—savings—will be forced down.

If the overconsuming countries of Europe and North America reduce their overconsumption, in other words, global rebalancing must involve China. Either China must raise its consumption rate commensurately, or global growth must turn negative, which would itself adversely affect China, the largest exporting nation in the world. Because China is by far the biggest source of global underconsumption, it is very hard to imagine a world that adjusts without a significant adjustment in China.[6]

This adjustment won't be easy, especially if Japan tries to resolve its excess debt problems by forcing up its savings rate, as it seems to be doing. To explain why, it is worth digging a little deeper into the trade constraints that China and the world face. China's current account surplus has declined sharply from its peak of roughly 10 percent of GDP in the 2007–2008 period to just under 3 percent of GDP. Over the next two years the forecast is, depending on whom you talk to, either that it will rise significantly, or that it will decline to zero and perhaps even run into deficit. China's Ministry of Commerce has argued the latter and the World Bank the former.

It is not obvious which way the surplus will go, but I would argue that, either way, it is going to be a very strained and difficult process for both China and the world. The Ministry of Commerce contends, as many others do, that the rapid contraction in the surplus since the 2007–2008 peak indicates that China is indeed rebalancing and will continue to do so without too much difficulty.

Figure 1. China's Savings and Investment Rates

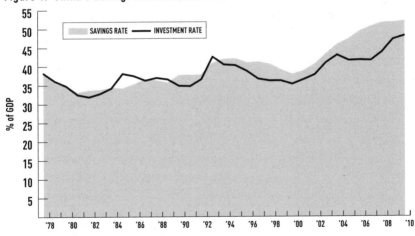

6 Jeffry A. Frieden, Michael Pettis, Dani Rodrik, and Ernesto Zedillo, *After the Fall: The Future of Global Cooperation*, Geneva Reports on the World Economy 14, 2012.

This is almost certainly wrong. China is not rebalancing, and the decline in the surplus was most likely driven wholly by external conditions. In fact, until 2011 the domestic imbalances got worse, not better. For proof, take a look at figure 1. It shows China's total savings rate as a share of GDP as well as China's total investment rate. Both numbers are extraordinarily high.

The current account surplus, of course, is equal to the excess of savings over investment—any excess savings must be exported, and by definition the current account surplus is exactly equal to the capital account deficit. This is the standard accounting identity that can be found in any economic textbook. As the graph shows, the last time investment exceeded savings in China was in 1993–1994, and during that time China of course ran a current account deficit. This was just before Beijing sharply devalued the renminbi, after which it immediately began running a surplus, which has persisted for seventeen years.

SAVINGS ARE RISING

From the accounting identity it is clear that if the current account surplus declines, there are logically only two ways it can happen. One way is for the savings rate to decline. In that case the investment rate must either rise or it must decline more slowly than the savings rate. The other way is for the savings rate to rise. In that case, the investment rate must rise even faster.

In the first case, a declining savings rate indicates that Chinese consumption is indeed rising as a share of GDP and that Chinese investment is declining (or at least rising more slowly than consumption). This is the "right" way for the trade surplus to decline because it represents a rebalancing of the Chinese economy away from its dependence on investment and the trade surplus and toward consumption. In the second case—the "wrong" way—consumption is actually declining further as a share of GDP, and the reduction in China's dependence on the trade surplus is more than matched by an increase in its dependence on investment.

From the graph it is perfectly clear that China did not rebalance after 2008. Rebalancing would require that domestic consumption rise. Again from the graph it is pretty clear that consumption's share of GDP has not increased since the onset of the crisis. If it had, the savings share of GDP would have declined.

Instead, savings continued to rise. This is the opposite of rebalancing, and it should not come as a surprise. Beijing has tried to increase the consumption share of GDP by subsidizing certain types of household consumption (white goods, cars), but because the subsidies are paid for indirectly by the household sector, as I will show in chapter 2, the net effect is to take away with one hand what is offered with the other. This is no way to increase consumption. As I will argue in this book, the only sustainable way to increase the consumption share of GDP is by increasing the household share of total wealth.

Meanwhile, investment continued to grow and, with it, debt continued to grow. Because the only way to manage all this debt is to continue repressing interest rates at the expense of household depositors, as I will show in chapters 2 and 3, households have to increase their savings rates to make up the difference. So national savings continue to rise.

What, then, explains the decline in China's current account surplus over the past three years? The graph makes it pretty obvious. The sharp contraction in China's current account surplus after 2007–2008 was driven by the external sector—the crisis caused demand to drop sharply as asset and real estate price declines reduced household wealth abroad—and in order to counteract the adverse growth impact, Beijing responded with a surge in investment in 2009. Analysts can argue whether this was an appropriate policy response (yes, because otherwise growth would have collapsed, or no because it seriously worsened the imbalances), but certainly since then as consumption has failed to lead GDP growth, investment has continued rising too quickly.

It is, therefore, rising investment, not rebalancing toward higher consumption, that explains the contraction in the current account surplus. The savings share of GDP was actually still rising through 2011.

So which way will China's current account surplus move over the next few years? If we could ignore external conditions, we would probably argue that the current account surplus should grow in the next few years. Why? Because Beijing is finding it impossibly hard to raise the consumption rate, and yet it is extremely important that it reduce the investment rate before debt levels become unsustainable. Under these conditions, we should expect the savings rate to hold steady as a share of GDP or—if we are lucky—for it to decline slowly over the next few years.

Investment, meanwhile, should decline quickly unless it proves difficult for the post-transition leadership to arrive at a consensus about the need to slow investment growth. We might in that case expect investment to begin dropping erratically sometime in 2013, but as of this writing it is unclear whether those within the leadership who understand how dire the economic situation is can convince the others during this period of the need to bring investment down sharply.

If investment rates drop more quickly than the savings rate, by definition this would result in an increase in China's current account surplus. This is why if we ignore external conditions we would probably predict a rise in China's trade surplus over the next few years. But, of course, there is a huge constraint here. Can the world accommodate China's need to absorb more foreign demand in order to help it through its own transition?

Here things seem unpromising. The first problem is that the big deficit countries have little appetite for rising imbalances. The United States, for example, wants to reduce its trade deficit, and at the very least it will resist a rapid increase in imports relative to exports. The deficit countries of peripheral Europe, which with the United States represent the bulk of global trade deficits during the past decade, will have to adjust quite quickly as the financial crisis continues and as their growth slows. Because all current account deficits must be financed externally, as the external financing available to peripheral Europe dries up and in fact turns to net capital outflows, their deficits will contract sharply and eventually become surpluses.

Of course, declining trade deficits around the world require declining trade surpluses. Part of the adjustment in Europe might well be absorbed by a contraction in Germany's surplus, but the Germans, concerned about their own rising debt, especially as a consequence of their tremendous bank exposure to peripheral Europe, are resisting as much as possible. They, too, are dependent for growth on absorbing foreign demand.

Certainly as a consequence of the crisis, Europe as a whole expects its trade surplus to rise. If instead it begins to run a large deficit, German growth will go negative and the debt burden of peripheral Europe will be harder than ever to bear. Europe, in other words, cannot be expected easily to accommodate China's need for a growing trade surplus. If foreign capital flows to Europe increase—perhaps as China and other the BRIC nations (Brazil, Russia, and India) and other large developing countries lend money to Europe—Europe's exports will certainly decline relative to imports. But because this means much slower growth for Europe, it isn't sustainable and would almost certainly worsen the European debt crisis.

THE PROBLEM OF JAPAN

A much bigger problem may be Japan, and it is surprising that few economists seem to be discussing the very adverse Japanese impact on the future development of global trade balances and its implications for China. Japan, as everyone knows, has an enormous debt burden that is made manageable only because it is financed domestically at extremely low rates. Here is Peter Tasker of the *Financial Times* on the subject:

> When Japan's bubble economy imploded in the early 1990s, public finances were in surplus and government debt was a mere 20 per cent of gross domestic product. Twenty years on, the government is running a yawning deficit and gross public debt has swollen to a sumo-sized 200 per cent of GDP.
>
> How did it get from there to here? Not by lavish public spending, as is sometimes assumed. Japan's experiment with Keynesian-style public works programmes ended in 1997. True, they had failed to trigger durable economic recovery. But the alternative hypothesis— that fiscal and monetary virtue would be enough—proved woefully mistaken. Economic growth had been positive in the first half of the lost decade, but after the government raised consumption tax in 1998 any momentum vanished. Today Japan's nominal GDP is lower than in 1992.[7]

Tokyo is clearly worried that it is running out of time to manage the debt, and indications are that it has finally become serious about reduc-

---

7   Peter Tasker, "Europe Can Learn From Japan's Austerity Endgame," *Financial Times*, February 12, 2012.

ing its debt burden. Of course any attempt to reduce the debt burden has implications for Japan's current account. The yen had already fallen substantially in anticipation of policies promised by the Liberal Democratic Party and its leader, Shinzo Abe, in the run-up to its victory in national elections in December 2012. What's more, Japan's current account surplus has already contracted substantially in the past two years, and in January 2012 it ran its biggest monthly trade deficit ever—$5.4 billion.[8]

This January deficit comes on the back of an overall 2011 trade deficit, the first time in decades that Japan has had an annual trade deficit. If Japan runs a current account deficit, of course, it means that Tokyo must turn to foreign sources to finance government debt since by definition a current account deficit implies that domestic savings are insufficient to fund domestic investment. This would be, for Japan, a very unwelcome prospect.

So how can Japan address its debt? One way is to ensure that the debt continues to be funded domestically, which means that Japan must force up its savings rate. It seems that Tokyo is planning to further raise taxes, especially consumption taxes, and to use the proceeds to pay down the debt. According to another article in the *Financial Times*:

> The government and the ruling Democratic party of Japan agreed on Friday on a draft plan to raise the country's controversial sales tax from 2014, taking a key step towards improving the country's stretched finances.
>
> Prime minister Yoshihiko Noda has faced an uphill struggle to convince some members of his own party, the opposition and the public that the tax is needed to help restore Japan's fiscal health at a time of global fears over sovereign debt. The tax has been opposed on the grounds that it could damage an already weak economy. The consumption tax, which is the government's most stable income stream at about a fifth of total revenues, has long been an obvious candidate for reform.[9]

---

8   Ben McLannahan, "Japan Posts Record Current Account Deficit," *Financial Times*, March 8, 2012.

9   Mure Dickie, "Japan Clears Hurdle to Consumption Tax," *Financial Times*, January 6, 2012.

In addition Tokyo and the business community are putting downward pressure on wages in order to increase the competitiveness of the tradable goods sector. In yet another article from the *Financial Times*:

> Bonuses have been coming under heavy pressure in Japan for years as part of a wider effort to restrain incomes. And while workers around the developed world have been complaining of a squeeze on incomes over the past two decades, in Japan thinner pay packets fuel wider deflation. That makes it even harder for the government to rein in its runaway debt and for the central bank to use monetary policy to boost growth.
>
> The National Tax Agency says average annual salaries, including bonuses, fell in nominal terms every year but one in the decade to 2010, sliding from ¥4.61m to ¥4.12m. The Japanese Trade Union Confederation (Rengo) says the average size of workers' bonuses has fallen from a peak of 4.27 times monthly salaries in 1992 to just 2.83 times in 2010.
>
> More recently, a faltering of Japan's recovery from its deep 2008–2009 slump is threatening to further tighten the screws. Total cash earnings for Japanese salaried workers were down 0.2 per cent in December compared with the previous year, while special payments, which are mainly winter bonuses, fell 0.3 per cent.[10]

This set of policies aimed at helping Tokyo manage its debt burden could turn out to be a problem for China and the world because raising consumption taxes and reducing wages will push up the Japanese savings rate substantially. Either action pushes the growth rate of disposable income down relative to GDP growth, and lower disposable income usually means lower consumption—which is the same as higher savings.

These policies will probably also reduce the investment rate. Lower Japanese consumption, after all, should reduce business profits and so reduce the incentive for expanding domestic production, while pressure for austerity should restrain or even reduce government investment. Japan's savings rate is likely to rise while its investment rate drops.

---

10 Mure Dickie, "Low Wages Compound Japan's Grim Prospects," *Financial Times*, February 14, 2012.

By definition, because the current account surplus is equal to the excess of savings over investment, more savings and less investment mean that Japan's current account surplus must rise. Japan, in other words, is planning to move backward in terms of rebalancing. Until 1990 Japan had the same problem that China did: its rapid growth was largely a function of policies that transferred wealth from the household sector to subsidize growth, as I will show is the case with China.

These policies—an undervalued currency, repressed interest rates, and low wage growth (which, of course, are the same policies as China's, as I will show in chapter 2)—restrained consumption and encouraged debt-fueled investment. This investment, we now realize, was wasted on a massive scale in the 1980s, and the eventual government absorption of all the associated debt caused government debt to rise.

After 1990 Japan began the slow rebalancing process. But rather than raise household income directly by privatizing assets and transferring wealth directly to the household sector, the Japanese did it by effectively having the government assume private sector debt (a process we will discuss further in chapters 6 and 7). This was politically much easier than privatizing and removing interest rate and capital allocation distortions, but it also meant much slower growth and burgeoning debt.

Now Japan is faced with the same difficult options that it faced twenty years ago and that China faces today. It can privatize government assets, or it can revert to consumption-constraining policies. But if it constrains consumption growth and does not replace consumption with a surge in investment, how can it possibly grow except through growth in the trade surplus? Domestic consumption, domestic investment, and the trade surplus are, after all, the only sources of demand growth for any economy.

So where does all this leave us? Of the two big trade deficit entities, neither the United States nor peripheral Europe can allow its deficit to rise, and we may even see, in the latter case, a sharp drop in the deficit. Of the three big surplus countries, Germany is reluctant to allow its surplus to decline by much, and certainly if it declines faster than the European deficits decline, Europe's debt crisis will be even worse.

China's surplus can decline only if we see a very improbable decline in its savings rate or a very unwelcome increase in its investment rate. Internal pressures are likely to cause the savings rate to hold steady or to decline slowly as the investment rate declines more quickly. And Japanese reluctance to solve its debt problems by selling off government assets to pay down the debt requires that it resolve them with an increase in the trade surplus.

The refusal of the surplus countries to play a part in allowing the world to adjust has its counterpart in the refusal of the United States in the 1920s to do the same. At the time the well-known New York banker, Otto Kahn, warned that "having become a creditor nation, we have got now to fit ourselves into the role of a creditor nation. We shall have to make up our minds to be more hospitable to imports."[11] But domestic U.S. policies in the 1920s made it very difficult for the United States to play its role, and as a consequence the same kinds of trade and capital flow imbalances were generated in the 1920s as had been generated in the decade leading up to the 2007–2008 crisis. These resulted, of course, in the terrible adjustment of the 1930s in which the very trade surplus nation that had refused to play its role in the rebalancing ended up, not coincidentally, suffering most from the resulting trade collapse.

We have a similar problem today, in which deficit countries are forced to contract and reverse their deficits while surplus countries refuse to reflate domestic demand sufficiently to convert their large surpluses into equally large deficits. Needless to say, this isn't going to work, and at least one of the above countries is going to be extremely disappointed. Historical precedents suggest that surplus countries are likely to be the most disappointed and will suffer most from the strains on international trade.

The "good" news is that if this conflict leads to much slower global growth, as it certainly will, the resulting reduction in commodity prices, including oil, will help absorb some of the changes in the trade imbalances as commodity-exporting countries see their exports fall sharply. But it is hard to see much other relief.

---

11 Jeffry A. Frieden, "Sectoral Conflict and Foreign Economic Policy 1914–1940," *International Organization* 42, no.1 (Winter 1998).

CHAPTER 2

CHINA'S DOMESTIC IMBALANCES[1]

In order to determine what policy choices China faces, I started with the two assumptions listed in the preceding chapter. The first assumption is that the fundamental imbalance in China is the very low GDP share of consumption. This low GDP share reflects a growth model that systematically forces up the savings rate mainly by repressing consumption growth (actually by repressing household income growth, which effectively accomplishes the same thing). As a consequence of this consumption-repressing growth model, Chinese growth is driven largely by the need to keep investment levels extraordinarily high.

Why? Because for any economy there are three sources of demand—domestic consumption, domestic investment, and net foreign consumption and investment (that is, the trade surplus). Growth in all three, however, is constrained by various factors.

China's trade surplus by the middle of the last decade was so high (the highest as a share of global GDP in more than one hundred years, and perhaps ever, depending on how we classify trade between Great Britain and its colonies in the late nineteenth century) that it could not reasonably be expected to generate much more growth in demand. Household consumption, meanwhile, was a relatively limited source of demand in China (representing little more than half the global average as a share of

---

1 Part of this chapter is based on my book *The Great Rebalancing: Trade, Conflict, and the Perilous Road Ahead for the World Economy* (Princeton, N.J.: Princeton University Press, 2012).

GDP). Because it was proving almost impossible to increase the household consumption share, for reasons we will discuss in the rest of this chapter, this left growth in investment as the main source of Chinese GDP growth.

There is a widespread conception that China is an export-led economy. It isn't. It is an investment-led economy, but because fundamental to its growth model are policies that systematically force up the savings rate—to levels even higher than the extraordinarily high investment rate—China must resolve domestic demand imbalances by exporting either the excess savings or the excess of what it produces over what it can consume or invest domestically. China's high trade surplus, in other words, is simply a residual that is necessary to keep investment-driven growth manageable under conditions of repressed domestic consumption.

What makes the process unsustainable, besides the limited foreign appetite for growing Chinese trade surpluses, is that the very high growth rate in investment—combined with skewed political incentives that heavily favor continued increases in investment regardless of the cost, and with significant pricing distortions, especially in the cost of capital—has resulted in overinvestment and an unsustainable increase in debt. I will show later in the chapter why this is the case, but the key point to remember is that only a rising consumption share of GDP can rebalance the economy away from its dependence on investment.

My second major assumption is that China must and will rebalance in the coming years. This rebalancing will take place either because the authorities take concrete steps to reverse the process that led to the imbalances, or, if they don't, the imbalances will lead to a debt crisis that will force rebalancing in a disorderly way. My reason for saying this, as discussed in chapter 1, is that global savings and investment must balance, and China can support an extraordinarily high savings rate only if the rest of the world has a correspondingly low savings rate. The fact that low savings countries are being forced to deleverage and to raise their domestic savings makes it impossible for China to maintain its high savings rate.

How plausible are these two key assumptions? The first assumption, that the fundamental imbalance in China is the very low GDP share of consumption, may have been controversial in some quarters as recently as two to three years ago, and there still are economists who disagree—for example, two Chinese academics, from Fudan University and the China Europe International Business School, both in Shanghai, who wrote in early 2013:

> This argument leads to our second point: consumption has been underestimated by official statistics. The true ratio could be 60–65 per cent—both normal and desirable for a fast-growing developing economy.
>
> There are several sources of error. First, housing consumption—at just 6 per cent of GDP—is seriously underestimated in view of exorbitant property prices. It makes up about 14 per cent in the bigger Organisation for Economic Co-operation and Development countries. According to our estimate, China's true rate is no less than 10 per cent.
>
> Second, official statistics do not account for private consumption paid for by companies and treated as business costs or investment expenditure. There is a great deal of this in China—for example, we suspect, most imported luxury cars. If such private consumption makes up, speaking conservatively, 10 per cent of household consumption, China's consumption rises by more than 3 per cent of GDP.
>
> The third source of underestimation relates to the household survey method. High-income households are known to be under-represented in the sample. And, as there are no explicit incentives to be accurate, participating households may easily fail to report some expenditures. In-kind consumption is often under-recorded or undervalued.[2]

We will see later in this book why these three arguments are muddled, irrelevant, and mistaken, respectively. Certainly, if consumption were truly such a high share of GDP it is hard to explain why small changes in the growth rate of credit (most of which goes to finance investment) would translate into such large changes in GDP growth. What matters at

---

2 Jun Zhang and Tian Zhu, "Chinese Shoppers Are Thriving," *Financial Times*, January 14, 2013.

any rate is not the classification of expenditures but the multiple relationships—the causal relationship between growth in debt and growth in reported GDP and the associated relationship between growth in debt and growth in debt-servicing capacity.

The important thing is that it has pretty much become accepted among most economists, and it has certainly been a formal part of Beijing's discourse, that consumption in China is dangerously low, and this of course has policy implications. Most analysts agree that at 34 to 35 percent of GDP, Chinese household consumption is incredibly low and must rise sharply.

To see why this is a problem, and how much household consumption must rise before it can be said to have been partially resolved, it is useful to discuss how we got there. Has Chinese growth been "unbalanced," and if so, in what sense is it unbalanced and how does that affect the trade account? Chinese growth is unbalanced because, as we discussed in the first chapter, the very rapid GDP growth generated especially in the past decade has relied too heavily on net exports and investment and too little on domestic household consumption.

The most striking expression of this imbalance is the declining share of GDP represented by household consumption. In the 1980s household consumption represented about 50 to 52 percent of GDP. This is a very low number, but it is not unprecedented. Globally, consumption represents roughly 65 percent of GDP. Consumption for most European countries lies in the 60 to 65 percent range. Consumption for other developing countries can easily fall in the 65 to 70 percent range—much of Latin America, for example, is within that range. Consumption in the United States has been around 70 to 72 percent in recent years, while consumption in parts of peripheral Europe before the crisis also reached this level or close to it.

By Asian standards, however, Chinese consumption in the 1980s was not exceptionally low. South Korean and Malaysian consumption has been around 50 to 55 percent of GDP for much of the past two decades (although during and after the Asian crisis, Malaysian consumption did drop to around 45 percent of GDP before recovering a year later). Other major Asian economies—India, Japan, Taiwan, and Thailand—show consumption in the range of 55 to 60 percent of GDP.

THE INVESTMENT PUMP

During the first decade of the reform period, Chinese consumption started at the low end of the range, even for low-consuming Asian countries. As the country grew during the 1990s Chinese consumption declined further as a share of GDP. By the end of the decade Chinese household consumption represented a meager 46 percent of GDP. This was not unprecedented—as I discuss above, Malaysian consumption, after all, had dropped to 45 percent a year after the 1997 crisis—but the Chinese consumption level was more typical of a country in crisis than of a country in ruddy good health.

But the story doesn't end there—in fact, the consumption share of GDP began to fall precipitously. By 2005, household consumption in China had declined to around 40 percent of GDP. With the exception of a few very special and unique cases, this level is unprecedented in modern economic history. Not surprisingly Beijing reacted to this very low number with a great deal of concern. Policymakers pledged during 2005 to take every step necessary to raise household consumption growth and to help rebalance the economy.

Why were they worried? Because, as we discussed earlier in this chapter, in any economy there are only three sources of demand: domestic consumption, domestic investment, and the trade surplus. If a country has a very low domestic consumption share, by definition it is overly reliant on domestic investment and the trade surplus to generate growth.

This meant that future Chinese growth was vulnerable. Policymakers, of course, cannot fully control the trade surplus, because this depends on the ability and willingness of the rest of the world to continue absorbing it. With the largest trade surplus ever recorded as a share of global GDP just before the onset of the global crisis—all the more astounding since the two previous record holders, Japan in the late 1980s and the United States in the late 1920s, were countries whose share of global GDP was two to three times China's share—it wasn't at all obvious that China could expect its trade surplus to increase much more.

Furthermore, there was also already a great deal of concern even by 2005 that China's high investment rate was proving unsustainable. Beijing had engineered extremely high and growing investment rates for the previous twenty-five years, and this made a great deal of economic sense at the beginning of the reform process, after 1978, when China was seriously and obviously underinvested for its level of development. But after so many years of furious investment growth, there were increasing worries that China had become overinvested, perhaps even massively overinvested, by the early and middle part of the decade.

We will discuss China's vulnerability to the trade surplus and investment more fully in chapters 3 and 5, but with consumption so low, it would mean that China was overly reliant for growth on two sources of demand that were unsustainable and hard to control. Only by shifting to higher domestic consumption could the country reduce its vulnerability and ensure continued rapid growth. This is why in 2005, with investment at a shockingly low 40 percent of GDP, Beijing announced its resolve to rebalance the economy toward a greater consumption share.

Not surprisingly, most observers, both foreign and Chinese, hailed Beijing's new resolve and excitedly reported that with these new initiatives the problem of low household consumption share was about to be addressed and fixed. There was a widespread perception that Beijing had always managed to achieve its economic targets and that this new economic target would also be dispatched with efficiency.

A few economists remained skeptical. They pointed out that previous policy successes had almost always involved targets—expanding the high-speed rail network, deepening transportation infrastructure, building ports, expanding manufacturing capacity, creating corporate champions—that could be addressed and resolved mainly by increases in investment. However, when the target involved an outcome that could not be determined by an increase in investment—slowing environmental degradation, reducing corruption, raising the income share of the poor, expanding the quality rather than the quantity of education—Beijing often failed to achieve its target.

The correct lesson, they argued, was not that Beijing was able to manage the economy efficiently, identify necessary objectives, and achieve them. It was that Beijing was able to increase investment whenever it wanted. Given low transparency, limited political accountability, and near-total control over interest rates, national savings, and the banking system, perhaps this should not have been a surprise.

But because rebalancing the economy toward consumption could not be achieved by mandating higher investment—on the contrary, it would require lower investment—it was not at all clear that Beijing's previous successes were relevant. The very different set of requirements needed to achieve success, the skeptics argued, would make the target much harder to achieve.

The skeptics further argued that a low and declining consumption share of GDP was not an accident. It is, in fact, fundamental to the growth model. And because it is fundamental to the growth model, Beijing would not be able to raise the consumption share of GDP without abandoning the investment-driven growth model altogether. Because there was as of yet no political consensus in favor of taking the necessary drastic steps, success was very unlikely. As a result the skeptics warned that consumption would barely grow from the 40 percent level for many years and might even stagnate further.

It turned out that even the skeptics underestimated the difficulty of the adjustment China was facing. For the next five years GDP growth continued to surge ahead of household consumption growth until 2011, the last year for which complete statistics are available, when household consumption declined to an astonishing 34–35 percent of GDP. This level is almost surreal. For all its determination, in other words, Beijing was not only incapable of reversing the downward trend in the household consumption share of GDP, but it could not even prevent a near-collapse.

The flip side of the decline in consumption, of course, has been the rise in household savings, which is simply the obverse of consumption. Part of the rise in savings has been the rise in household savings. After bouncing around erratically between 10 percent and 20 percent of disposable income in the 1980s, by 1990 Chinese household savings equaled 12 to 15 percent of disposable income. Around 1992 household savings began rising steadily until 1998, and then stabilized at around 24–25 percent until very recently, when they rose slightly to about 26 percent of disposable income.

GROWTH MIRACLES ARE NOT NEW

But this is not the whole story—household savings are only part of total national savings. The real increase in national savings in China in recent years was caused by the sharp increase in corporate and government savings. It is worth pointing out, though, that corporate savings, and even government savings, are themselves caused by the transfer from household income via low interest rates and other hidden subsidies funded ultimately by the household sector, as we shall see later.

Rising savings, of course, must have an impact on the current account balance. Because the current account is equal to the excess of savings over investment, a rapid rise in savings must have as its counterpart a rapid rise in the current account surplus.

This is exactly what happened. China ran small surpluses or deficits on the trade account during the three-decade period until 1996, when it booked its last trade deficit. A steady upward march of its trade surplus then ensued, and by 2003, the trade surplus was around 5 percent of China's GDP. After 2003 the trade surplus surged to over 10 percent of GDP in 2007–2008, before coming down sharply in 2009 and 2010 as a result of the global crisis.

Investment, too, rose steadily during this period as a share of GDP, as indeed it had to if the growth model were going to work. In 1990 it was around 23 percent of GDP. It rose sharply in 1992–1994 to around 31 percent of GDP, stabilized at that level, and then began climbing inexorably around 1997–1998 to reach 50 percent in 2011. The level would be even higher if we include, as we should, imported commodities that are stockpiled.

Rising investment, rising savings, and rising trade surpluses are inextricably linked in China's case, and nothing suggests the impressiveness of the increase in the national savings rate as much as the fact that China was able to combine a soaring investment rate with a soaring trade surplus. Because the trade surplus is a function of the excess of savings over investment, a high and soaring investment rate is normally associated with a declining trade surplus, or even (and more normally) a large and rising trade deficit.

This is what happened, for example, in the United States during the nineteenth century, when very high domestic investment rates exceeded domestic savings, and the United States had to import foreign capital, mainly from Great Britain and the Netherlands, for most of the century. As the obverse, of course, the United States also ran trade deficits for most of the nineteenth century until the 1880s, when the combination of its huge earlier investment in capacity, rising income inequality (which limits consumption growth), and the impact of the 1873 crisis on ordinary household income began generating trade surpluses.

Yet China, with an even higher investment rate, one of the highest in history, and rapidly rising asset values (which should goose household wealth and, with it, consumption) was forced nonetheless to run an extraordinarily high trade surplus. The only way this could happen is if the savings rate were even more extraordinarily high.

And it was, but why? I will discuss later in this chapter the many policies, ranging from undervalued currencies, to lagging wage growth, to financial repression, to environmental degradation and weakening social safety nets as policies or institutional structures that encouraged very rapid growth but at the expense of the household share of that growth. All of these occurred in China to an exaggerated extent, and it was for these reasons that Chinese savings soared.

These growth strategies engineered by Beijing forced households to subsidize investment and production, thus generating rapid economic and employment growth at the expense of household income growth. It is the lagging growth in household income that has primarily constrained household consumption growth.

This is borne out by the numbers. From 1990 to 2002, household income ranged from 64 percent of GDP to 72 percent. It peaked in 1992 before a tremendous bout of inflation in 1993 and 1994 brought it down, and it then began a slow, erratic descent to 66 percent in 2002. After that it plunged to less than 50 percent of GDP, if the numbers can be believed (most analysts assume that there is substantial hidden income in China, especially among the wealthy and very wealthy, that is not captured in the official surveys).[3]

If there were a way to measure changes in wealth—such as the value of the deteriorating social safety nets and the degrading environment, the

---

3   It is worth noting that because the wealthy consume a smaller share of their income than others, if there is indeed hidden income, and if this accrues mostly to the wealthy, China's savings rate may be even higher, and its consumption rate even lower, than the official numbers. This seems to be one of the confusions found in the *Financial Times* op-ed piece cited at the beginning of this chapter.

present value of savings as interest rates are changed for policy reasons, and so on—and household income were adjusted by these changes, I suspect the decline would have been greater. Certainly that is what the savings numbers imply.

But with Chinese household consumption and household income growing so rapidly in the past decade, around 7 to 8 percent annually, why has it been so difficult to raise the consumption share of GDP and reduce China's overwhelming dependence on a growing trade surplus and especially accelerating investment to generate growth? To understand the causes of China's great imbalance, it is necessary to consider the development model that generated its tremendous growth in the past two decades.

There is nothing especially Chinese about the Chinese development model. It is mostly a souped-up version of the Asian development model, probably first articulated by Japan in the 1960s. The Japanese development model was itself a variation on what in the early part of the nineteenth century was referred to as the "American System," which was itself formalized as the "National System" by the important and unfairly neglected nineteenth-century German economist Friedrich List, who had spent 1825 to 1830 in exile in the United States.[4]

There are three main components of the American System, much of which was first thought out and articulated by the brilliant first U.S. secretary of the Treasury, Alexander Hamilton, in his three Reports to the Congress: the First Report on the Public Credit, the Report on Manufactures, and the Second Report on the Public Credit. These three main components are (1) infant industry tariffs (to encourage the development of domestic manufacturers until they are able to compete with more productive foreign manufacturers), (2) internal improvements (that is, infrastructure investment), and (3) a sound system of national finance (aimed at providing capital to local businesses).[5]

One of the leading proponents of the American System was Pechine Smith, who in 1872 moved to Japan to advise the Tokyo government on

---

4   See, most importantly, Friedrich List, *The National System of Political Economy* (London: Longmans, Green, and Company, 1841).

5   Michael Lind, *Land of Promise: An Economic History of the United States* (New York: HarperCollins, 2012), 107.

its modernization program. He helped set out the basic framework that became known as the Japanese or the East Asian development model. This development model eventually shared many characteristics with the American System, with two important differences.

First, while the American System aimed to protect U.S. manufacturers in their infant stage from excessive foreign competition, its practitioners were not in favor of the development of national champions. On the contrary, they encouraged domestic competition on the understanding that it was competition, not protection, that drove innovation and productivity growth. Without such growth in innovation and productivity, U.S. manufacturers would never be able to compete efficiently with foreign producers.

Second, and more important, the American System was developed in opposition to the then-dominant economic theories of Adam Smith and David Ricardo, in part because classic British economic theory seemed to imply that reductions in wages were positive for economic growth by making manufacturing more competitive in the international markets. A main focus of the American System was to explain what policies the United States, with its much higher wages than in Europe at the time, had to engineer to generate rapid growth. Sustaining high wages, in fact, became one of the key aspects of the American System.[6]

The Japanese version of this development model, as well as many of the various versions implemented in other countries throughout the twentieth century, shared its view of wages not with the American System but with classic British economic theory. Rather than take steps to force up wages and keep them high—thereby both driving productivity growth and creating a large domestic consumption market for American producers—the later versions of the American System sought to repress growth in household income relative to total production as a way of improving international competitiveness. This is perhaps the main reason that the

---

6 One of the best books on the workings and development of the American System is Michael Hudson, *America's Protectionist Takeoff 1815–1914* (ISLET, 2010), especially after pages 29 and 160. Like most of Michael Hudson's work, this book is original, unorthodox, historically grounded, and filled with provocative ideas that have much to say about economic development and sustainable growth.

United Sates, unlike other countries that have implemented similar development strategies in the twentieth century, tended to run large current account deficits for many years.

This different focus on whether high wages are to be encouraged or discouraged is, as far as I know, discussed very little in the theoretical literature. But I believe this different focus is nonetheless the most important distinguishing factor between the American development model and its many descendants in the twentieth and twenty-first centuries. I will not develop a framework for this argument in this book, but I will argue that one consequence of this difference is that growth in demand tends to be more sustainable when it is balanced between growth in both consumption and investment.

The main point here is that contrary to much public perception, China's growth model is neither unique nor new, and it is possible to understand a great deal about its functioning and its prospects by examining earlier versions. The growth model shares fundamental features with a number of periods of rapid growth—for example, Germany during the 1930s, Brazil during the "miracle" years of the 1960s and 1970s, and the USSR in the 1950s and 1960s, when most informed opinion (including, apparently, President Kennedy) expected the country to overtake the United States economically well before the end of the century. While these policies can generate tremendous growth early on, they also lead inexorably to deep imbalances.

At the heart of the various investment-driven growth models are massive subsidies for manufacturing and investment aimed at generating rapid growth and the building up of infrastructure and manufacturing capacity. These subsidies make it very cheap to increase investment in manufacturing capacity, infrastructure, and real estate development, generating enormous growth in employment, and they allow investors, whether private or, more typically, the state, to generate great profitability.

THE BRAZILIAN MIRACLE

But, of course, all subsidies must be paid for by someone, and in nearly every case they are paid for by the household sector. In some cases, as with the Brazilian investment-driven miracle in the 1960s and 1970s, the household costs are explicit. Brazil taxed household income heavily and invested the proceeds in manufacturing and infrastructure. In doing this it managed to achieve eye-popping growth rates.

This is not necessarily a bad strategy. Brazil achieved extraordinary growth in the late 1950s and 1960s and with it, income levels rose quickly. But as demonstrated by the history of every investment-driven growth miracle, including that of Brazil, high levels of state-directed subsidized investment run an increasing risk of being misallocated, and the longer this goes on the more wealth is likely to be destroyed even as the economy posts high GDP growth rates. Eventually the imbalances this misallocation created have to be resolved and the wealth destruction has to be recognized.

What's more, with such heavy distortions imposed and maintained by the central government, there is no easy way for the economy to adjust on its own. Growth in Brazil was not capable of being sustained except by rising debt, and by the mid-1970s Brazil reached its domestic debt capacity limit, as loans simply could not be repaid out of earnings.

Fortunately for the administration of President Ernesto Geisel—but perhaps unfortunately for Brazil—the contraction of domestic debt capacity coincided with the petrodollar crisis. As oil prices soared during the crisis, international banks had to recycle rapidly rising dollar earnings from Organization of Petroleum Exporting Countries (OPEC) nations even as they saw few opportunities to deploy these earnings in Europe and the United States, which were then suffering from economic stagnation.

The petrodollars were recycled in massive amounts to developing countries, including Brazil, that were able to continue funding high levels of wasteful investment and maintain GDP growth, even with the oil price shocks of the 1970s, at nearly 6 percent. But even the external funding had its limits, and by 1981–1982 after the accompanying debt levels proved to be a limit to further expansion, Brazil spent much of the 1980s, its famous lost decade, reversing the growth that occurred during its miracle years. Debt, as we will learn over the next few years in China, has always been the Achilles' heel of the investment-driven growth model.

There are, however, some important differences between the various forms of the investment-driven growth model. The Asian or Japanese variety relies on less explicit taxation mechanisms to accomplish the same purpose of subsidizing investment. Rather than confiscate household wealth through high income taxes, as the Brazilian version of the model did, three much more indirect mechanisms are used for the same effect.

First, wage growth is constrained to well below the growth in worker productivity. In China, for example, worker productivity has grown much faster than wages, especially during the past decade, when workers' wages have slightly more than doubled while productivity nearly tripled.

There are many reasons for the gap between the two. One reason may have to do with the huge pool of surplus labor in the countryside available to compete for jobs, thereby keeping wages low. There are also other, policy-related reasons that limit wage growth. Workers are not able to organize except in government-sponsored unions that see things more from the point of view of employers than of workers. Migrant workers are also unable to get residence permits, called *hukou*, and without *hukou* what limited protection workers may have is sharply reduced since living in an urban area without the proper *hukou* is tolerated but technically illegal.

The important thing to remember from the growth model perspective is that, whatever the reason, lagging wage growth in China represented a transfer of wealth from workers to employers. An increasing share of whatever workers produced, in other words, accrued to employers, and this effective subsidy allowed employers to generate excess profit or cover losses. The fact that productivity grew much faster than wages acted like a growing tax on workers' wages, the proceeds of which went to subsidize employers.

It is important to remember the impact this hidden tax has on the relationship between GDP growth and household income growth. By effectively subsidizing employers at the expense of workers, it boosted the competitiveness of businesses, increased overall production, and constrained household income, and with it, household consumption.

The second mechanism common among Asian development model countries for transferring income from households to manufacturers is an undervalued exchange rate, as we also have already discussed. Most analysts acknowledged that after the massive devaluation of the renminbi in 1994, followed by soaring productivity (which increases the real undervaluation of a currency), the renminbi was seriously undervalued for much of the past two decades.

It is not wholly meaningful to discuss by how much the renminbi was undervalued because any undervaluation of the currency must be considered in conjunction with the other transfers that had similar impacts on the trade balance. Most economists, however, have estimated the undervaluation to be anywhere from 15 to 30 percent, which, given long-term changes in productivity and inflation, is probably a reasonable if imprecise estimate.

Clearly this represents a significant undervaluation. The undervaluation of the exchange rate, remember, is a kind of consumption tax imposed on all imported goods, and everyone in China who is a net importer—which includes all households except perhaps subsistence farmers—must pay this very large implicit tax.

POWERING GROWTH

Chinese manufacturers in the tradable goods sector, heavily concentrated in Guangdong and the coastal provinces, receive the opposite "negative" tax, or subsidy, in the form of lower domestic costs relative to higher foreign prices for their goods. Again we must remember the impact this hidden consumption tax has on the relationship between GDP growth and household income growth. By raising the cost of foreign imports, it puts downward pressure on real household income in China.

But by subsidizing Chinese exporters, thus increasing their competitive strengths relative to foreign competitors, the undervaluation of the renminbi boosts domestic production. An undervalued exchange rate is simply another powerful mechanism for increasing the gap between what a country produces and what it consumes. This not only affects the trade account, but if high GDP growth is created through high investment growth, an undervalued currency also creates domestic imbalances in the way growth is generated.

The third mechanism for creating the domestic imbalances, and probably by far the most powerful, is financial repression. Economist Carmen Reinhart describes financial repression this way:

> One of the main goals of financial repression is to keep nominal interest rates lower than would otherwise prevail. This effect, other

things being equal, reduces governments' interest expenses for a
given stock of debt and contributes to deficit reduction. However,
when financial repression produces negative real interest rates and
reduces or liquidates existing debts, it is a transfer from creditors
(savers) to borrowers and, in some cases, governments.

This amounts to a tax that has interesting political-economy
properties. Unlike income, consumption or sales taxes, the "repression" tax rate is determined by factors such as financial regulations
and inflation performance, which are opaque if not invisible to the
highly politicized realm of fiscal policy. Given that deficit reduction usually involves highly unpopular spending cuts and/or tax
increases, the "stealthier" financial-repression tax may be a more
politically palatable alternative.[7]

The "invisibility" of the financial repression tax, of course, is one of
its most important features—and one most welcome by fiscal authorities
everywhere. The Chinese financial system is severely repressed. Almost
all household savings in China are in the form of bank deposits, and the
banks are controlled by the monetary authorities, who determine the
direction of credit, socialize the risks, and set interest rates.[8]

In China, the central bank, the People's Bank of China, following the
instructions of the State Council, sets both the maximum deposit rate,
above which banks cannot pay, and the minimum lending rate, below
which they cannot lend. Because the central bank sets both rates very
low, it is effectively transferring a large share of resources from depositors
to borrowers.

How large a share? In the past decade nominal lending rates have
averaged little more than 6 percent even as the economy grew nomi-
nally by 14 to 16 percent annually. Even if we accept that annual GDP
growth has been overstated by 2 to 3 percentage points, it still implies
that borrowers received a hugely disproportionate share of growth at the
expense of depositors.[9] With lending rates 4 to 8 percentage points below

---

7   Carmen Reinhart, "Financial Repression Back to Stay," Bloomberg, March 12, 2012.

8   Nicholas Lardy, *Sustaining China's Economic Growth After the Global Financial Crisis*
    (Washington, D.C.: Peterson Institute for International Economics, 2012).

9   If capital is indeed being misallocated and wasted in China, it should show up in

adjusted GDP growth rates, and with household deposits (including farm deposits) equal to anywhere from 80 to 100 percent of GDP, the total transfer from households to state-owned enterprises, infrastructure investors, and other favored institutions amounts to anywhere from 3 to 8 percent of GDP annually.

In addition, in China, as in many of the countries that followed the Asian development model, not only have interest rates been set extremely low, but the minimum spread between the deposit rate and the lending rate is set very high, thereby guaranteeing the banks a large, and very safe, profit. This also comes at the expense of depositors. Using the same methodology as above, we can estimate the additional transfers to be roughly equal to 1 percent of GDP. In a country where household income accounts for approximately 50 percent of GDP, these combined interest-rate-related transfers, of 4 to 9 percent of GDP, represent a very high hidden tax on households. A recent International Monetary Fund (IMF) paper, using a different methodology, similarly calculates the effective cost of the transfer to be at least 4 percent of GDP.[10]

Depositors, however, cannot opt out. There are significant restrictions on their ability to take capital out of the country, and for the most part only the very rich can exploit foreign investment opportunities. Nor are there are many domestic investment opportunities. Local stock and bond markets are rudimentary, highly speculative, and rife with insider activity—which effectively transfers profits from non-insiders to insiders while leaving the former with the full risk.

In China, there are few other legal and safe alternatives to the banking system. The most common alternatives include real estate and the so-called informal banking sector, both of which generally have very high

---

the form of rising nonperforming loans in which realized losses would effectively reduce GDP growth by the amount of the write-off. Because rather than recognize nonperforming loans, the banking system resolves them implicitly by continuous debt forgiveness as the loans are rolled over at artificially low interest rates, these losses are simply postponed into the future and GDP growth is not adjusted to the lower number. I estimate that this results in GDP growth overstatement by at least 2 to 3 percentage points annually.

10 Il Houng Lee, Murtaza Syed, and Liu Xueyan, "Is China Over-Investing and Does It Matter?" IMF Working Paper 12/277, November 2012.

transaction costs and limited liquidity, so neither is a useful investment alternative for depositors with limited means or who may need to be able to access their savings quickly.

Depositors, in other words, have little choice but to accept very low deposit rates on their savings, which are then transferred through the banking system to banks and borrowers who benefit from these very low rates. Very low lending and deposit rates create a powerful mechanism for using household savings to boost growth by heavily subsidizing the cost of capital.

And remember yet again the impact that this hidden tax on savings has on the relationship between GDP growth and household income growth. By lowering borrowing costs substantially, it encourages investment, primarily in real estate development, infrastructure building, and of course in manufacturing capacity (in China there is very little consumer financing).

But by reducing the amount of interest income depositors receive, the hidden tax reduces the overall income they should be earning, and this is especially noticeable in a country where savings are so high and income so low as a share of GDP. This is certainly a powerful mechanism for increasing the gap between what a country produces and what it consumes

As an aside, the resulting low, or even negative, cost of capital for Chinese borrowers explains the seeming paradox of China's capital-intensive, rather than labor-intensive, growth. Ask most people what China's comparative advantage is, and they are likely to say that it is the huge pool of cheap and disciplined labor. But in fact this doesn't seem to be reflected in the economy. If China's comparative advantage were cheap labor, we would expect its growth to be heavily labor-intensive as businesses loaded up on the most efficient input.

But China's growth is actually heavily capital-intensive. It is in fact among the most capital-intensive in the world and far more so than any other developing country—even countries that are far richer and with higher wage levels. Chinese businesses behave, in other words, not as if labor is the cheapest input they have but rather as if capital were the cheapest input. They are right. Labor may be cheap, but for most large borrowers capital is free or may even have a negative cost.

THE COST OF SUBSIDIES

All three of these mechanisms—lagging wage growth, an undervalued currency, and repressed interest rates—do the same thing, albeit by distributing the costs and benefits in different ways to different groups among households and producers. They effectively tax household income and use the proceeds to subsidize producers, infrastructure investors, real estate developers, local and provincial borrowers, central government borrowers—anyone, in fact, who has access to bank lending, who employs workers, or who manufactures tradable goods, whether or not the goods are actually exported.

In principle these mechanisms are no different than the mechanism used by Brazilians during their "miracle" years. Brasília heavily taxed household income and used the proceeds to promote industrialization and growth. Beijing does the same thing, but the taxes are hidden. The only real difference is that after 1975–1976, when domestic borrowing capacity had become constrained, Brazil turned to external financing—subsidized by government guarantees—to fund investment. As a result, the impact of net foreign capital inflows meant that Brazil exported a portion of its domestic demand through a current account deficit, which perhaps accounts for the slowdown in growth relative to the early miracle years.

Besides the ones we have discussed, there are many other such hidden taxes in China. Environmental degradation, a serious problem with China's growth model, is an important transfer of income from households to businesses. Likewise, energy and water subsidies (including the cost of building facilities), the deterioration in the social safety net once provided by work units, subsidized land sales, ease of eminent domain expropriations, and so on are all forms of tax and subsidy.

Not surprisingly, these enormous transfers have made it very profitable for governments, businesses, and real estate developers to invest in infrastructure and productive capacity, even if the real returns on the projects did not justify the costs. In so doing they ignited an investment boom.

The result of this enormously successful model is so much investment-driven and employment-generating growth that even with massive transfers from households, household income has nonetheless surged. In

China, for the past decade as the country was clocking in growth rates of 10 to 12 percent annually, household income, and with it household consumption, grew 7 to 9 percent annually.

In a sense it seems like a free lunch. Household income is taxed heavily in order to generate tremendous growth. This growth causes employment to surge, and as workers move from subsistence living in rural China to the factories and development sites of the cities, their income surges. So rapidly does household income grow that even after the huge hidden taxes are deducted, the wealth and ability to consume of the average Chinese grows at a pace that is the envy of world. So why not continue this growth model forever?

Because the model cannot be sustained. There are at least two constraints: the first has to do with investment, and the second with the external account.

To address the first constraint, in the early stages for most countries that have followed the investment-driven growth model, when investment is low, the diversion of household wealth into investment in capacity and infrastructure is likely to be economically productive. After all, when capital stock per person is almost nonexistent, almost any increase in capital stock is likely to drive worker productivity higher. When you have no roads, even a simple dirt road will sharply increase the value of local labor.

The longer heavily subsidized investment continues, however, the more likely that cheap capital and socialized credit risk will be used to fund economically wasteful projects. Dirt roads quickly become paved roads. Paved roads become highways. And highways become superhighways with eight lanes in each direction. The decision to upgrade is politically easy to make because each new venture generates local employment, rapid economic growth in the short term, and opportunities for fraud and for what economists politely call "rent-seeking behavior," while the costs are spread across the entire country through the banking system and over the many years during which the debt is repaid (and most debt is rolled over continuously).

It also seems easy to justify intellectually the infrastructure upgrades. After all, rich countries have far more capital stock per person than poor countries, and those investments were presumably economically justified, so, according to this way of thinking, it will take decades of continual upgrading before China comes close to overbuilding.

The problem with this reasoning, of course, is that it ignores the economic reason for upgrading capital stock and assumes that capital and infrastructure have the same value everywhere in the world. They don't. Worker productivity and wages are much lower in China than in the developed world. In addition, weak social capital and the current institutional framework discourage the most productive use of resources (it is hard to set up businesses in China, good connections are a greater cause for success than efficiency, legal structures are complex, local governments regularly intervene for non-economic reasons, innovation is discouraged, and on and on).

This means that the economic value of infrastructure in China, which is based primarily on the value of wages it saves, is a fraction of the value of identical infrastructure in the developed world. It makes no economic sense, in other words, for China to have levels of infrastructure and capital stock comparable to those of much richer countries because this would represent wasted resources—like exchanging cheap labor for expensive, labor-saving devices.

Of course, because risk is socialized—that is, all borrowing is implicitly or explicitly guaranteed by the state—no one needs to ask whether the locals can use a highway and whether the economic wealth created is enough to repay the cost. The system creates an acute form of what is sometimes called the "commonwealth" problem. The benefits of investment accrue over the immediate future and within the jurisdiction of the local leader who makes the investment decision.

The costs, however, are spread widely through the national banking system and over many years, during which time, presumably, the leader responsible for the investment will have been promoted to another post in another jurisdiction. With very low interest rates and other subsidies making it hard to determine whether investments actually reduce value or create it, the commonwealth problem ensures that further investment in infrastructure is always encouraged.

The problem of overinvestment is not just an infrastructure problem. It occurs just as easily in manufacturing. When a manufacturer can borrow money at such a low rate that it effectively forces most of the borrowing cost onto household depositors, the manufacturer doesn't need to create economic value equal to or greater than the cost of the investment. Even factories that systematically destroy value can show high profits if the interest rate subsidy is large enough. And there is substantial evidence to suggest that China's state-owned sector in the aggregate has probably been a massive value destroyer for most if not all of the past decade but is nonetheless profitable thanks to hidden subsidies provided by households.[11]

At some point, in other words, rather than create wealth, capital users begin to destroy wealth, but they nonetheless show profits by passing more than 100 percent of the losses onto households. The very cheap capital especially means that a very significant portion of the cost—as much as 20 to 40 percent of the total amount of the loan—is forced onto depositors just in the form of low interest rates.[12] This is effectively a form of debt forgiveness granted, unknowingly, by depositors.

Under these circumstances, it would take heroic levels of restraint and understanding for investors not to engage in value-destroying activity. This is why countries following the investment-driven growth model— like Germany in the 1930s, the USSR in the 1950s and 1960s, Brazil in the 1960s and 1970s, Japan in the 1980s, and many other smaller countries—have always overinvested for many years leading, in every case, either to a debt crisis or a "lost decade" of surging debt and low growth.[13]

---

11 A mainland think tank, the Unirule Institute of Economics, estimated in 2011 that monopoly pricing and direct subsidies may have accounted for 150 percent or more of total profitability in the state-owned sector over the past decade. Repressed interest rates may have accounted for an additional 400 to 500 percent of total profitability over this period. Monopoly pricing, direct subsidies, and repressed interest rates all represent transfers from the household sector.

12 Artificially lowering a coupon on a ten-year loan by 4 percentage points represents debt forgiveness equal to 25 percent of the loan. Lowering the coupon by 6 percentage points represents forgiveness of 35 percent of the loan. Although most bank loans in China have maturities of less than ten years, these loans are rarely repaid and are instead rolled over for very long periods of time, increasing the value of the implicit debt forgiveness.

13 The German experience, of course, ended in war, and not in a debt crisis, but according to Yale historian Adam Tooze, the German invasion of eastern Europe occurred three to four years earlier than the military command was prepared for largely because the country was almost insolvent and could not afford to wait any longer. See Adam Tooze, *The Wages of Destruction: The Making and Breaking of the Nazi Economy* (London: Allen Lane, 2006).

THE TRADE IMPACT

The second constraint is that policies that force households to subsidize growth are likely to generate much faster growth in production than in consumption—growth in household consumption being largely a function of household income growth. In that case even with high investment levels, large and growing trade surpluses are needed to absorb the balance because, as quickly as it is rising, the investment share of GDP still cannot increase quickly enough to absorb the decline in the consumption share.

This is what happened in China in the past decade until the crisis in 2007–2008, after which Beijing had to engineer an extraordinary additional surge in investment in order to counteract the contraction in the current account surplus. As Chinese manufacturers created rapidly expanding amounts of goods, the transfers from the household sector needed to subsidize this rapid expansion left them unable to purchase a constant share of the goods being produced. The result was that China needed to export a growing share of what it produced, and this is exactly what it did, especially after 2003.

As long as the rest of the world—primarily the United States and the trade deficit countries of Europe—have been able to absorb China's rising trade surplus, the fact that domestic households absorbed a declining share of Chinese production didn't matter much. A surge in American and European consumer financing allowed those countries to experience consumption growth that exceeded the growth in their own manufacture of goods and services.[14]

But by 2007 China's trade surplus as a share of global GDP had become the highest recorded in one hundred years, perhaps ever, and the rest of the world found it increasing difficult to absorb it. To make matters worse, the global financial crisis sharply reduced the ability and willingness of other countries to maintain current trade deficits, and as we will see, this downward pressure on China's current account surplus is likely to continue.

---

14 Thomas I. Palley, *From Financial Crisis to Stagnation: The Destruction of Shared Prosperity and the Role of Economics* (Cambridge: Cambridge University Press, 2012). See especially chapter 6.

So China has hit both constraints—capital is wasted, perhaps on an unprecedented scale (this constraint in fact may have been hit a decade or more ago), and the world is finding it increasingly difficult to absorb excess Chinese capacity. For all its past success, China now urgently needs to abandon the development model because debt is rising furiously and at an unsustainable pace. Once China reaches its debt capacity limits, perhaps in four to five years, growth will inexorably come crashing down.

CHAPTER 3

IS OVERINVESTMENT A PROBLEM?

The second of the two key assumptions that I listed in chapter 1—that China will necessarily rebalance in the next few years—is, I think, very plausible. In fact, over the long run it is actually more than just plausible. It is an arithmetical certainty, because it can be violated only if China has unlimited borrowing capacity and the world has unlimited appetite for rising China trade surpluses. Of course, neither of those possibilities is realistic.

Where some analysts might disagree with my second assumption is on the issue of timing. Some analysts continue to argue that there isn't yet a significant overinvestment problem in China, which implies that debt is not rising at an unsustainable pace, or if it is, that it can continue rising for many more years before the debt burden itself becomes unsustainable.

This also implies that the consumption imbalance is temporary and can resolve itself gradually and over time as the benefits of earlier investment begin to emerge and eventually overwhelm the total costs of those investments. Of course, if this is true, China does not need a surging current account surplus because if investment isn't being wasted, China can keep investment rising faster than savings for many more years. The current account surplus, remember, is just the excess of savings over investment.

The argument that capital has been misallocated on an extraordinary scale in China during the past decade or two has been surprisingly controversial, at least until very recently. Those who have argued against the thesis acknowledge that there has been some waste, but they contend that wasted investment in China is no different from wasted investment in any other economy and that there is no reason to charge China with excess.

For example, Arthur Kroeber of Gavekal Dragonomics Research, one of the more cogent of the China bulls, has long argued that investment levels in China, far from being too high, are actually too low, and he adds that concerns about an unsustainable debt buildup are consequently exaggerated. In a February 2011 research report, he said:

- GDP will grow at 8 percent a year in 2010–2020; growth will remain investment intensive though not as much as in the past decade

- High investment can continue because the capital stock is relatively low and urbanization is only half done

- Overall debt level is not high and bank cash flows can absorb a rise in bad loans; management of SOE and sovereign debt under rising interest rates will be a challenge[1]

The *Economist* has also been among the most regular proponents of the argument that China does not suffer from significant investment misallocation and that in fact investment levels in China are extremely low:

China is a poor country in the early stages of development. Its high investment-to-GDP ratio is often flagged as evidence of overinvestment, yet its capital stock per person is only 5 per cent of America's or Japan's. As for overcapacity, most of last year's investment boom went into infrastructure, not manufacturing. Unlike Japan, which built "bridges to nowhere," China really does need more infrastructure. Nor is the country on the verge of financial crisis—and even if share and house prices do collapse, the result is likely to be a pause, not a prolonged period of Japanese-style stagnation.[2]

Part of the reason for the confusion about whether China's investment levels are too high, of course, is the mistaken—and altogether too common—comparison of investment levels and capital stock between China

---

1 Arthur Kroeber, *China's Next Decade*, Gavekal Dragonomics Research, February 2011.
2 "China's Battered Image: Bears in a China Shop," *Economist*, January 14, 2010.

and the United States and Japan. China is one of the poorest countries in the world, with very low wages and low worker productivity; the United States and Japan are among the richest countries in the world, with very high levels of worker productivity. By American and Japanese standards, of course Chinese investment levels are low, but then so are investment levels in every poor or middle-income country in the world.

To argue that China cannot have overinvested until its per capita capital stock is nearly comparable to that of the United States or Japan is tantamount to saying that overinvestment is conceptually impossible in countries that are not already very rich, something that is demonstrably false. Latin America's lost decade of the 1980s, after all, was a crisis caused mainly by many years of rapidly rising debt and misallocated investment, and yet many of the countries that suffered during the crisis were extremely poor.

In fact, poor countries are more, not less, likely to suffer from overinvestment. Since the purpose of investment is to increase worker productivity, and the value of productivity increases tends to be lower in countries with very low levels of productivity and weak institutional frameworks than in countries with very high levels of productivity and more robust institutional frameworks, poor countries should have optimally much lower capital stock than rich countries. What's more, when capital stock is low, it is often easier for the (often politically well-connected) beneficiaries of high investment spending to justify investment above these low optimal levels, simply by arguing that capital stock is low.

But to propose that investment misallocation in China does not vary qualitatively or systemically from that of other economies implicitly assumes a comparable investment allocation process. This assumption is mistaken for at least three reasons. These have to do with the way investment decisions are made and the relationship between investment conditions and the allocation process.

First, severe distortions in pricing mechanisms, especially in the cost of capital, interfere with the capital allocation process in China. The cost of capital is set artificially low and may have even been negative in real terms for much of the past decade.

This matters, because in any system in which the price of capital is set artificially low or high, it does not take irrational investors to misallocate capital. On the contrary, rational investors will systematically invest in projects that are not economically viable in the former case, or reject projects whose economic returns exceed their cost in the latter case. For this not to be the case requires a superhuman decisionmaking process, of which there is little evidence in China.

Second, there are in China significant distortions in the distribution of costs and benefits that create very strong incentives for investment misallocation. Broadly speaking, there are two types of distortions. The first consists of a process in which the benefits of any investment (higher growth, lower unemployment, opportunities for rent-seeking behavior) accrue largely to the jurisdiction in which the investment takes place, while the costs are spread throughout the national banking system. The second distortion in incentives occurs over time. The benefits of any investment accrue over the investment period, while the costs accrue over the debt repayment period. Because loans are rarely repaid and are instead rolled over for many years, the costs are ultimately spread out over ten to fifteen years after the investment is completed.

Under these conditions it would require, once again, a superhuman and irrational investment decisionmaking process for the system not to tend toward overinvestment. Economists are very aware of the impact of these kinds of distorted incentive structures in pork-barrel policies elsewhere in the world, but it is a little strange to assume, as many do, that this process cannot take place in China in spite of overwhelming evidence that it does.

THE INVESTOR BASE

And finally, the structure of the investor base in China is another factor that prevents the capital allocation process from functioning in China. One of the sources of financial instability in the past crisis has been the nature of investor behavior, and so it makes sense to discuss how and under what conditions investors can be a destabilizing influence on the market.

Investors make buy and sell decisions for a wide variety of reasons, and when there is a good balance in the structure of their decisionmaking, financial markets are stable and efficient. But there are times in which investment is heavily tilted toward a particular type of decision, and this can undermine the functioning of the markets.

To see why this is so, it is necessary to understand how and why investors make decisions. An efficient and well-balanced market is composed primarily of three types of investment strategies—fundamental investment, relative value investment, and speculation—each of which plays an important role in creating and fostering an efficient market.

Fundamental investment, also called value investment, involves buying assets in order to earn the economic value generated over the life of the investment. When investors attempt to project and assess the long-term cash flows generated by an asset, to discount those cash flows at some rate that acknowledges the riskiness of those projections, and to determine what an appropriate price is, they are acting as fundamental investors.

Although most economics textbooks limit their discussions of the investment decisionmaking process to this kind of decisionmaking, in fact not all investment decisions are of this nature. Relative value investing, which includes arbitrage, involves exploiting pricing inefficiencies to make low-risk profits. Relative value investors may not have a clear idea of the fundamental value of an asset, but this doesn't matter to them. They hope to compare assets and determine whether one asset is over- or underpriced relative to another, and if so, to profit from an eventual convergence in prices.

Finally, speculation is an investment strategy that takes advantage of information that will have an immediate effect on prices by causing short-term changes in supply or demand factors that may affect an asset's price in the hours, days, or weeks to come. These changes may be only temporary and may eventually reverse themselves, but by trading quickly, speculators can profit from short-term expected price changes.

Each of these investment strategies plays a different and necessary role in ensuring that a well-functioning market is able keep the cost of capital low, absorb financial risks, and allocate capital efficiently to its more productive use. A well-balanced market is relatively stable and allocates capital in an efficient way that maximizes long-term economic growth.

Each of the investment strategies also requires very different types of information, or interprets the same information in different ways. Speculators are usually "trend" traders, or trade against information that can have a short-term impact on supply or demand factors. They typically look for many opportunities to make small profits. When speculators buy in rising markets or sell in falling ones—either because they are trend traders or because the types of leverage and the instruments they use force them to do so—their behavior, by reinforcing price movements, adds volatility to market prices.

DIFFERENT INVESTORS MAKE MARKETS EFFICIENT

Value investors typically do the opposite. They tend to have fairly stable target price ranges based on their evaluations of long-term cash flows discounted at an appropriate rate. When an asset trades below the target price range, they buy; when it trades above the target price range, they sell.

This brings stability to market prices. For example, when higher-than-expected GDP growth rates are announced, a speculator may expect a subsequent rise in short-term interest rates. If a significant number of investors have borrowed money to purchase securities, the rise in short-term rates will raise the cost of their investment and so may induce them to sell, which would cause an immediate but temporary drop in the market. As speculators quickly sell stocks ahead of them to take advantage of this expected selling, their activity itself can force prices to drop. Declining prices put additional pressure on those investors who have borrowed money to purchase stocks, and they sell even more. In this way, the decline in prices can become self-reinforcing.

Value investors, however, play a stabilizing role. The announcement of good GDP growth rates may cause them to expect corporate profits to increase in the long term, and so they increase their target price range for stocks. As speculators push the price of stocks down, value investors become increasingly interested in buying until their net purchases begin to stabilize the market and eventually reverse the decline.

Arbitrage, or relative value, investors or traders play a different role. Like speculators, they tend not to have long-term views of prices. However, when any particular asset is trading too high (low) relative to other equivalent risks in the market, they sell (buy) the asset and hedge the risk by buying (selling) equivalent securities.

A well-functioning market requires all three types of investors for socially beneficial projects to have access to cheap capital. Value investors allocate capital to its most productive use. Speculators, because they trade frequently, provide the liquidity and trading volume that allows value investors and relative value traders to execute their trades cheaply. They also ensure that information is disseminated quickly.

Arbitrage, or relative value trading, forces pricing consistency and improves the information value of market prices, which allows value investors to judge and interpret market information with confidence. It also increases market liquidity by combining several different, related assets into a single market. When the buying of one asset forces its price to rise relative to that of other related assets, for example, relative value traders will sell that asset and buy the related assets, thus spreading the buying throughout the market to related assets. It is because of relative value and arbitrage strategies that we can speak of a unified market for different assets.

Without a good balance of all three types of investment strategies, financial systems lose their flexibility, the cost of capital is likely to be high, and the markets become inefficient at allocating capital. This is the case, for example, in a market dominated by speculators. Speculators focus largely on variables that may affect short-term demand or supply for the asset, such as changes in interest rates, political and regulatory announcements, or insider behavior.

They ignore information like growth expectations or new product development whose impact tends to reveal itself only over long periods of time. In a market dominated by speculators, prices can rise very high or drop very low on information that may have little to do with economic value and a lot to do with short-term, non-economic behavior.

Value investors keep markets stable and focused on profitability and growth. For value investors, short-term, non-economic variables are not an important or useful type of information. They are more confident of their ability to discount economic variables that develop and affect cash flows over the long term. Furthermore, because the present value of future cash flows is highly susceptible to the discount rate used, these investors tend to spend a lot of effort on developing appropriate discount rates. However, a market consisting of only value investors is likely to be illiquid and pricing-inconsistent. This would cause an increase in the required discount rate, thus raising the cost of capital for borrowers.

Because each type of investor is looking at different information, and sometimes analyzing the same information differently, investors pass different types of risk back and forth among themselves, and their interaction ensures that a market functions smoothly and provides its main social benefits. Value investors channel capital to the most productive areas by seeking long-term earning potential, and speculators and arbitrage traders keep the cost of capital low by providing liquidity and clear pricing signals.

WHERE ARE THE VALUE INVESTORS?

Not all markets have an optimal mix of investment strategies. China, for example, does not have a well-balanced investor base. There is almost no arbitrage trading because this requires low transaction costs, credible data, and the legal ability to short securities. None of these is easily available in China.

There are also very few value investors in China because most of the tools they require, including good macro data, good financial statements, a clear corporate governance framework, and predictable government behavior, are missing. As a result, the vast majority of investors in China tend to be speculators. One consequence of this is that local markets often do a poor job of rewarding companies for decisions that add economic value over the medium or long term. Another consequence is that Chinese markets are very volatile, and this raises the cost of capital for business.

Why are there so few value investors in China and so many speculators? Some experts argue that this is because of the lack of investors with long-term investment horizons, such as pension funds, that need to invest money today for cash flow needs far off in the future. Others argue that very few Chinese investors have the credit skills or the sophisticated analytical and risk-management techniques necessary to make long-term investment decisions. If these arguments are true, increasing the participation of experienced foreign pension funds, insurance companies, and long-term investment funds in the domestic markets, as Beijing has done, certainly seems like a good way to make capital markets more efficient.

But the issue is more complex than that. China, after all, already has natural long-term investors. These include insurance companies, pension funds, and, most important, a very large and remarkably patient potential investor base in its tens of millions of individual and family savers, most of whom save for the long term. China also has a lot of professionals who have trained at leading U.S. and UK universities and financial institutions, and they are more than qualified to understand credit risk and portfolio techniques. So why aren't Chinese investors stepping in to fill the role provided by their counterparts in the United States and other rich countries?

The answer lies in what kind of information can be gathered in the Chinese markets and how the discount rates used by investors to value this information are determined. If we broadly divide information into "fundamental" information, which is useful for making long-term value decisions, and "technical" information, which refers to short-term supply and demand factors, it is easy to see that the Chinese markets provide a lot of the latter and almost none of the former. The ability to make fundamental value decisions requires a great deal of confidence in the quality of economic data and in the predictability of corporate behavior, but in China today there is little such confidence.

Furthermore, regulated interest rates and pricing inefficiencies make it nearly impossible to develop good discount rates. Finally, a very weak corporate governance framework makes it extremely difficult for investors to understand the incentive structure for managers and to be confident that managers are working to optimize enterprise or market value.

And yet, when it comes to technical information useful to speculators, China is too well endowed. Insider activity is very common in China, even when it is illegal. Corporate governance and ownership structures are opaque, which can cause sharp and unexpected fluctuations in corporate behavior. Markets are illiquid and fragmented, so determined traders can easily cause large price movements. In addition, the single most important player in the market, the government, is able—and very likely—to behave in ways that are not subject to economic analysis.

This has a very damaging effect on undermining value investment and strengthening speculation. In the first place, unpredictable government intervention causes discount rates to rise, because value investors must incorporate additional uncertainty of a type they have difficulty evaluating.

Second, it puts a high value on research directed at predicting and exploiting short-term government behavior, and thereby increases the profitability of speculators at the expense of other types of investors. Even credit decisions must become speculative, because when bankruptcy is a political decision and not an economic outcome, lending decisions are driven not by considerations of economic value but by political calculations.

VALUE INVESTORS PULL OUT OF CHINA TELECOM

A dramatic example of the impact of government behavior on value investing was the initial public offering of China Telecom stock in November 2002. The offering was scheduled to come out at a time of weak international demand, and there was some concern that the transaction might not be as successful as hoped. Because this was a politically important transaction, the Chinese government pushed through a large and unexpected increase in international interconnection fees in an attempt to bolster demand for the shares. The idea was that it would result in higher profits for the company.

But instead of boosting demand for the stock, the action actually had the effect of reducing demand. The deal, originally expected to raise more than $3 billion, ended up raising only $1.4 billion, even after being priced at the bottom of the expected price range.

Why was the deal so unpopular among investors? Part of it had to do with weak global markets at the time of launch. But the final sudden slump in demand came about largely because the government's actions made clear that it would allow political factors to affect the company's profitability. Value investors, who dominate the large international markets, felt that their ability to judge the long-term profitability of China Telecom had suddenly been compromised. They saw that the company's profitability depended not on economic factors, which they are able to judge, but on political factors, which they cannot. As a consequence, they raised their discount rate—that is, they lowered the price at which they were willing to buy shares.

The government's action not only hurt the China Telecom issue, but, more broadly, it also weakened investors' confidence in their ability to "understand" Chinese companies. Ironically, the government action strengthened speculative behavior by reducing the role of value investing. This example indicates one of the main problems facing the development of local capital markets. China is attempting to improve the quality of financial information in order to encourage long-term investing, and it is trying to make markets less fragmented and more liquid. But although these are important steps, they are not enough. Value investors need not just good economic and financial information, but also a predictable framework in which to derive reasonable discount rates. And here China has a problem.

There are several factors, besides the poor quality of information, that cause discount rates to be very high. These include market manipulation, insider behavior, opaque ownership and control structures, and the lack of a clear regulatory framework that limits the ability of the government to affect economic decisions in the long run. This forces investors to incorporate too much additional uncertainty into their discount rates.

Chinese value investors, consequently, use high discount rates to account for high levels of uncertainty. Some of this uncertainty represents normal business uncertainty. This is a necessary component of an economically efficient discount rate, since all projects have to be judged not just on their expected return but also on the riskiness of the outcome. But Chinese investors must incorporate two other economically inefficient sources of uncertainty. The first is the uncertainty surrounding the quality of economic and financial statement information. The second is the large variety of non-economic factors that can influence prices.

This is the crucial point. It is not just that it is hard to get good economic and financial information in China. The problem is that even when information is available, the variety of non-economic factors that affect value force the appropriate discount rate so high that value investors are priced out of the market.

Speculators, however, are much more confident about the value of the information they use. Furthermore, because their investment horizon tends to be very short, they can largely ignore the impact of high implicit discount rates. As a result, it is their behavior that drives the whole market. One consequence is that capital markets in China tend to respond to a very large variety of non-economic information and rarely, if ever, respond to estimates of economic value.

During the past decade, Beijing was betting that increasing foreign participation in the domestic markets would improve the functioning of the capital markets by reducing the bad habits of speculation and increasing the good habits of value investing and arbitrage. But it has become pretty clear that this faith was misplaced: the market is as speculative and inefficient as ever.

This should not have been a surprise. The combination of very weak fundamental information and structural tendencies in the market—such as heavy-handed government interventions and market manipulation—reward speculative trading and undermine value investing. This forces all investors to focus on short-term technical information and to behave speculatively. In China even Warren Buffett would speculate.

All investors in Chinese markets must be speculators if they expect to be profitable. As long as this is the case, investors will not behave in a way that promotes the most productive capital allocation mechanism in the market, and such efforts as bringing in foreigners will have no meaningful impact.

What China must do is something radically different. It must downgrade the importance of speculative trading by reducing the impact of non-economic behavior from government agencies, manipulators, and insiders. It must improve corporate transparency. It must continue efforts to raise the quality of both corporate reporting and national economic data. Finally, it must deregulate interest rates and open up local markets to permit arbitragers to enforce pricing consistency and to allow better estimates of appropriate discount rates.

If done correctly, these changes would be enough to spur a major transformation in the way Chinese investors behave by permitting them to make long-term investment decisions. It would reduce the profitability of speculative trading and increase the profitability of arbitrage and value investing, and so encourage a better mix of investors. If China follows this path, it would spontaneously develop the domestic investors that channel capital to the most productive enterprise. Until then, China's capital markets, like those of many countries in Latin America and Asia, will be poor at allocating capital.

THE SYSTEM TENDS TOWARD CAPITAL MISALLOCATION

In the end, even without specific evidence, there are many reasons to assume that Chinese financial markets are unlikely to allocate capital efficiently:

- An artificially low cost of capital must necessarily distort the use of capital. Rational businesses will always tend to maximize the use of their cheapest and most efficient inputs, and if the price of one of those inputs is artificially lowered, a rational business will of course increase its use of that input. The very low cost of capital means that Chinese businesses that have access to capital will automatically use more than would otherwise be justified.

  If the externalities provided by the investment are sufficiently positive, this overuse of capital may nonetheless be rational from a national standpoint, but we should not simply assume that externalities are always sufficiently positive. More important to the case of China, we must recognize that even if the externalities were sufficiently positive at some point, over time their value must decline as cheap capital is continuously deployed. In that case, artificially low interest rates are no longer rational for the country as a whole.

- The same is true for other subsidies, which are substantial in China—both in the case of direct subsidies, such as cheap energy, monopoly pricing power, or subsidized land, and the case of indirect subsidies, like low environmental protection costs or cheap labor caused by discrimination against certain classes of migrant workers. These subsidies distort the use of inputs to production. As in the case of financial repression, the distortions are not always value destroying. If the externalities associated with higher distorted production are high enough, the subsidies can be justified as welfare enhancing. If not, they are value destroying.

- Investment incentives are distorted. One way in which they are distorted is in the diffusion of costs and benefits over jurisdictions. The benefits of an investment accrue to the jurisdiction in which the investment occurs, while the costs are spread out through the national or provincial banking system. In that case, it may be rational to engage in value-destroying investment.

- A second way in which incentives are distorted is by the diffusion of costs and benefits over time. The benefits of an investment occur during the time of the investment and the immediate aftermath. The costs of the investment are spread out over the debt repayment period, which usually occurs over ten to twenty years. In that case, again, it may be rational to engage in value-destroying investment.

- A third way in which incentives are distorted is in widespread corruption, which creates an extreme case of what economists refer to as the "agency" problem. It leads to investment decisions that are driven more by the need to maximize corruption opportunities than to maximize value creation. This problem is reinforced by a lack of accountability and transparency.

- Most lending to local governments, state-owned enterprises, and large manufacturers is implicitly or explicitly guaranteed by the state. Because banks are also implicitly guaranteed by the state, and most Chinese believe that both formal deposits in the banking system as well as those "dis-intermediated" deposits known as "wealth management products" are guaranteed by the banks, there is an automatic tendency within the financial system that profits are privatized and losses socialized. It is very difficult to find any case in economic history in which a system of privatized profits and socialized losses has not resulted in excessive risk-taking in speculative ventures.

- Credit has expanded at an extraordinary speed during most of the past decade and especially in the past four years. What's more, the fastest expansion has taken place in new and largely unregulated sectors of the financial markets. The hard-to-understand wealth management products, for example, rose in three years from a negligible amount to nearly 50 percent of GDP. The chairman of the Bank of China said in late 2012 that China, which represents about 11–12 percent of the global economy, accounted for 40–50 percent of total money creation in the last three years.[3]

There are few, if any, precedents in history in which such a rapid rise in credit and money was not associated with a surge in bad lending. Even recent Chinese history (during the 1990s, for example, at the end of which 40 percent of all loans were estimated to be nonperforming) suggests a strong link between the two.

- The lack of reliable macro data, a stable regulatory framework, and a clear corporate governance framework creates an enormous disadvantage for investors trying to invest for value. At the same time, the importance of inside information and sudden changes in government behavior encourage short-term investment thinking.

- The classic nineteenth-century arguments of Karl Marx, J. A. Hobson, and Charles Arthur Conant suggest that rising income inequality is a major source of instability because it forces up the domestic savings rate while reducing legitimate opportunities for domestic investment (the rich consume less, so rising income inequality means consumption grows more slowly than income). This causes excess savings, according to the classical view, to flow into both imperialist expansion (the export of capital) and speculative investment.

- In China, what may matter more is the rising state share of total income. A rising state share of total income also forces up the savings rate while reducing the growth of domestic investment opportunities, and so has the same net impact as rising income inequality. It forces excess savings to be either exported or invested in speculative ventures.[4]

My argument in this chapter is that the structure of the Chinese economy and financial system makes it especially vulnerable to problems

---

3 Xiao Gang, "Commentary: Regulating Shadow Banking," *People's Daily*, October 12, 2012.

4 For more on the relationship between the savings and household income shares of GDP, see chapter 1 of Michael Pettis, *The Great Rebalancing: Trade, Conflict, and the Perilous Road Ahead for the World Economy* (Princeton N.J.: Princeton University Press, 2013).

of capital misallocation. This doesn't prove, of course, that China must have misallocated capital on a substantial scale. But unless we can identify specific factors within the Chinese financial system that protect it from making the same kinds of investment mistakes that have been made in similar cases elsewhere, it will be very difficult to believe that capital misallocation has not occurred. (That is notwithstanding the assumption that many foreign analysts seem to have that some sort of superhuman decisionmaking process is involved.).

But as strong as the theoretical case may be, there are also many more practical reasons for arguing that China has misallocated capital substantially. In chapter 4 I will discuss the impact of financial repression on investment misallocation. Chapter 5 will look at more specific evidence that investment is indeed being misallocated.

MONETARY POLICY UNDER FINANCIAL REPRESSION

B efore continuing with the discussion about why China must and will rebalance its economy toward a greater consumption share of GDP, it is worth digressing for an examination of the consequences and implications of financial repression in China. Financial repression is not only at the heart of China's rapid growth and its economic imbalances, but it also explains a number of otherwise puzzling aspects of the Chinese development model. In many ways this may be the most theoretically interesting chapter of this book, but readers who have no interest in monetary policy may skip it because its relevant conclusions will be repeated later—in fact, they have already been implicitly put forward in chapter 2.

I will argue in this chapter that a repressed financial system will seem to operate in a fundamentally different way than a market-based financial system, but in fact the principles under which it operates can be explained using what we already know about the operations of monetary policy in a market-based financial system. I should point out that except for a few brief discussions and references in some of my earlier writings, I believe that this may be the first time these principles have been analyzed and set out, at least in the context of developing economies, and this may be why many analysts have been confused by or have misunderstood a number of consequences of Chinese monetary policy.[1]

---

1 Two of the first important texts to discuss financial repression comprehensively are Edward S. Shaw, *Financial Deepening in Economic Development* (New York: Oxford

One of the apparent puzzles about China's growth trajectory, especially in the past decade, is the seeming disconnect between rapid monetary growth and relatively stable domestic inflation. It is well known in economic theory that countries that have open capital accounts are forced to choose between managing the currency regime and managing domestic monetary policy. When a central bank chooses to intervene in the currency to maintain a desired exchange level, the amount of money it creates domestically is largely a function of the need to monetize net inflows or outflows. When it chooses to manage the domestic money supply, the supply and demand for that currency in the international markets will determine the value of the currency.

In China's case the capital account is technically closed, so in principle Beijing should be able to manage both the value of the currency and the amount of domestic liquidity. In reality, however, there are two significant limits to the country's ability to maintain closed capital accounts. First, and most obviously, the capital account is the obverse of the current account, and any country with the volume of exports and imports that China runs (not to mention its enormous current account surpluses for much of the past decade) will experience significant activity in the capital account. Although much of this is controlled by the central bank, an increasing share of capital flows occurs outside the central bank.

Second, China has extensive trading borders, a great deal of local corruption, and a long history both of capital control and capital control evasion. Throughout history, countries with large trading borders, wide-scale corruption, and a long history of capital control have rarely been able to control capital flows. That's because these factors undermine the ability of financial authorities to manage flows, and China is not an exception. In fact, during the past decade, China has experienced significant amounts of both speculative inflows and capital flight, measuring probably in the hundreds of billions of dollars. Neither of those is compatible with the strict enforcement of capital controls.

For all practical purposes, in other words, and in spite of formal capital flow restrictions, China is also forced to a greater or lesser extent

---

University Press, 1973), and Ronald I. McKinnon, *Money and Capital in Economic Development* (Washington, D.C.: Brookings Institution Press, 1973).

to choose between managing its currency regime and managing domestic money creation. Clearly, it has chosen to manage the currency regime: the enormous changes in central bank reserves—which at more than $3 trillion are the largest hoard of central bank reserves ever amassed by a single country—are a testament to that.

Monetary policy from the point of view of the balance of payments is pretty clearly a consequence of the central bank's need to monetize an enormous amount of net inflows. China's current account surplus began surging around 2003–2004 to levels that are almost unprecedented in history. At its peak, the current account surplus was up to 10 percent of China's GDP and equivalent to just over 1 percent of global GDP, one of the highest current account surpluses as a share of global GDP ever recorded.

The impact of the current account surplus on capital flows tended to reinforce monetary creation in at least two ways. As money poured into the country as a consequence of its current account surplus and its net surplus on the capital account (among other things, China is the largest recipient of foreign direct investment in the world), it helped ignite a credit-fueled asset boom, especially in the real estate sector. That encouraged additional speculative inflows looking to take advantage of soaring prices.

In addition, the massive current account surplus contributed to speculation about the trajectory of the renminbi. As investors expected the value of the renminbi to rise as it adjusted to current account inflows, even more speculative inflows poured into the country seeking to benefit from any appreciation. The result was that until late 2011, substantial net capital inflows boosted the already very high current account surplus, driving up central bank purchases to extraordinary levels.

As a share of global GDP, the only comparable hoard of foreign currency reserves occurred in the United Sates in the late 1920s. That period was distorted by the destruction of much of Europe's manufacturing capacity in World War I and by the impact that political uncertainty in Europe had in driving capital to the relative safety of the United States. During this time, when the United States experienced both massive current account surpluses and massive private capital account surpluses that generated its huge central bank reserve hoard, the U.S. share of global GDP was roughly three to four times the current Chinese share, which gives a sense of just how extraordinary the Chinese accumulation of reserves has been.

With so much money pouring into the country, the People's Bank of China was forced regularly to monetize an amount equal to a substantial share of its existing money base. Normally central banks would try to sterilize this money creation, and the People's Bank of China did try to mop it up. But most measures of money nonetheless continued to increase rapidly, and there is anyway a real question about the effectiveness of sterilization with highly liquid and credible instruments that are already a close substitute for money. The tools used to sterilize inflows—mainly short-term bills issued by the central bank—are themselves forms of money. The more extensively they are employed, the more liquid they become, and hence the more "money-like."

The alternative to a real and effective sterilization is for the Chinese economy to adjust in the form of a surge in inflation. As the money supply grows in response to China's current account surplus and net capital inflows, it should cause prices and wages to surge, forcing a real appreciation in the currency, until China's current account surplus and net capital account inflows both wither away.

This is, of course, the classic currency adjustment mechanism under the gold standard. As reserves soared in China, money creation soared along with it. Rapid money creation should have resulted in a rapid rise in domestic wages and prices as demand for goods and services outstripped supply. Rising domestic prices should have in turn undermined Chinese exports, encouraged imports, and reversed capital inflows.

But that didn't happen. In fact, during the past decade, price inflation in goods and services in China has been fairly moderate, and wages actually grew more slowly than productivity. Not only was China's export competitiveness not eroded by domestic money creation, as it would have been under the classical adjustment mechanism, but it also had, by some measures, even increased during this period. There have been periods during which inflation seemed about to take off, but these periods tended to be short-lived and were always followed by sharp declines in inflation.

At first this might seem to imply that sterilization was indeed effective in preventing money creation in China from getting out of hand. By selling central bank bills, transacting in the repo market, and raising minimum reserve requirements aggressively (to around 20 percent, compared with the 5–10 percent that is more common in developing countries), the central bank seems to have been successful in mopping up the money created by the monetization of current and capital account inflows. In doing so, it seems to have protected the Chinese economy from the normal consequence of maintaining an undervalued currency.

I will argue that what happened was, in fact, very different. Generally speaking, a number of countries besides China have managed to combine tremendous capital and current account inflows, rapid growth in foreign currency reserves, and low inflation for long periods. Japan in the 1980s is an example of that. There and in nearly every other case, these countries also had severely repressed financial systems.

What's more, although it was hard to find evidence of rapid money creation in changes in consumer prices in China (and in other similar countries), other parts of the economy behaved in ways that did seem consistent with rapid money creation. Credit, both inside and outside the formal banking system, grew astonishingly quickly, and, as usually occurs under conditions of too-rapid credit growth, credit standards deteriorated. The stock and real estate markets experienced bubble-like behavior. Producer prices rose rapidly. Global commodity prices, spurred largely by soaring Chinese demand, also soared.

BIFURCATED MONETARY EXPANSION

So was Chinese monetary expansion excessive, or, to put it differently, why is it that what seemed by most measures to be an extraordinary surge in money creation did not also result in significant wage and consumer price inflation? The answer, I will argue, has to do with the nature of money growth in financially repressed economies. Because the Chinese financial system is so severely repressed, money growth in China cannot be compared to money growth in a market-based financial system. Monetary growth is effectively bifurcated and affects producers and consumers in very different ways.

In saying that monetary growth is bifurcated, all I mean is that nominal money growth showed up as different rates of money growth for different parts of the economy. More specifically, the rate of monetary growth for producers exceeded the rate for consumers, and this becomes clear by measuring, on different sectors within the economy, the monetary impact of monetary expansion under financial repression.

Countries with significant financial repression can experience periods of rapid monetary expansion with results that do not conform to normal expectations precisely because of this bifurcation in the monetary impact of credit creation. On the production side of the economy, it is easy to see in China over the past decade what looked like the consequence of rapid monetary expansion—rapid growth in credit, rising productive capacity, surging production of manufacturing goods, asset bubbles, and other indicators.[2]

On the demand side of the economy, however, and especially considering household consumption, one gets a very different view—monetary expansion seemed to have been very subdued. Chinese household consumption typically grew much more slowly than GDP, and its share of GDP declined steadily. Consumer price inflation also tended to be low or moderate even in the face of what seemed like rapid monetary expansion.

So has there been too-rapid monetary expansion in China during the past decade or not? Why do some sectors seem to indicate that there has been, and other sectors that there hasn't? The answers depend, it turns out, on which economic sector we examine, and whether that sector was a net borrower or a net lender. We will see that financial repression can create a bifurcation in monetary expansion when

> a.) net savers and net borrowers are two very distinct groups, in this case, the former being households and the latter being producers of goods and infrastructure, including manufacturers, governments, real estate developers, and infrastructure investors; and

> b.) the bulk of savings consists of deposits in the banking system, and the bulk of corporate financing consists of bank lending or other forms of bank financing.

---

2 The production of services, meanwhile, grew much more slowly than the production of manufactured goods, which further reinforces this idea of a bifurcation in the money supply. Services are largely produced for domestic consumption, while manufactured goods are produced for domestic and foreign consumption and for domestic and foreign investment.

The experience of China (and other financially repressed economies) suggests that when interest rates are set artificially low in such a financial system, any given nominal expansion in money supply creates a lower real expansion in money on the consumption side and a higher real expansion in money on the production side. The consequence may be rapid GDP growth, a surge in investment, and low inflation for many years, but it also leads to sharply unbalanced growth in which the role of domestic demand as a driver of growth shrinks.

To see why, assume a country in which the "natural" nominal interest rate is 5 percent for all maturities. For the sake of simplicity, we will assume that deposit and lending rates are the same and that the marginal reserve requirement is constant, although these assumptions do not affect our final conclusions in any significant way.

Now let us assume that there are two simultaneous transactions. In one, a saver deposits $100 in the bank for one year at 5 percent interest. The $100 is immediately lent to a borrower for one year at 5 percent interest. One year from now, the saver will receive $105 and the borrower will repay $105.

In the other transaction, we assume that another saver deposits $97 for one year at 5 percent interest and that the money is immediately lent to a borrower for one year at 5 percent interest. For the sake of simplicity, we will round off the pennies and assume that in this case, the depositor receives $102 one year later and that the borrower repays $102.

It is clear that because of the first transaction the money supply has increased by $100, and the depositor will receive and the borrower will repay $105 in one year. It is also clear that because of the second transaction the money supply has increased by $97, and the depositor will receive and the borrower will repay $102 in one year.

But now let us posit that the central bank decides suddenly and arbitrarily to reduce both the deposit and lending rate to 2 percent. This has nothing to do with a change in inflationary expectations or the real demand for money—it is simply driven by other domestic considerations.

Following that decision, a third, less fortunate saver decides to deposit $100 for one year at 2 percent interest, and this $100 is immediately lent to a lucky borrower for one year at 2 percent interest. Which of the first two transactions is closer in its monetary impact to the third transaction?

From the depositor's point of view, the present value of $102 one year from now is only $97 (for simplicity, I am rounding off adjustments to the nearest dollar). Although the nominal amount of his deposit is $100, just like that of the first depositor, the real value of his deposit, discounted at the appropriate rate, is really only $97, just like that of the second depositor. If we define money so as to include deposits, did the money supply rise by $97 or $100?

On a comparable basis it is pretty clear that the third depositor's position, after interest rates were artificially lowered, is no different than that of the second depositor who deposited $97. Nominally the value of his deposit is the same as that of the first depositor, or $100, but his wealth is the same as that of the second depositor, or $97. Since it is real wealth, and not nominal deposits, that ultimately matters to the depositor, and which will affect his consumption and savings decisions, the third depositor is likely to behave over the long run as if he were in the position of the second depositor.

Because in this case a $100 deposit results in a $97 increase in the real value of deposits, in other words, it turns out that the nominal growth in money as measured by deposits overstates the real growth. Under financial repression a $100 transfer from the household to the bank in the form of a $100 bank deposit results in a smaller real deposit than under conditions of no financial repression.

If financial repression distorts the balance sheet of the depositor, what does it do to the balance sheet of the borrower? For the third borrower, who in our example borrowed under conditions of repressed interest rates, the transaction is the opposite of the depositor's transaction. The third depositor effectively had $3 "confiscated" from his assets in the form of an arbitrary reduction in the deposit rate. This $3 is transferred automatically to the borrower, so that the third borrower's liability more closely resembles that of the second borrower, even though he receives upfront the same $100 as the first borrower.

The nominal increase in money as measured by loans, in other words, understates the real increase. The third borrower receives both the $100 loan and a $3 "gift" in the form of partial forgiveness of his debt. His purchasing power has gone up not by $100 but by $103, even as the purchasing power of the third depositor has gone up by only $97.

TRANSFERS CHANGE THE MONETARY IMPACT

Depositors in a financially repressed system may make the same initial deposits as depositors in a non-financially repressed system and borrowers in a financially repressed system may receive the same initial disbursements as borrowers in a non-financially repressed system, but their resulting balance sheets are very different. Wealth is effectively transferred from the depositor to the borrower under financial repression, and so the purchasing power of the former is reduced relative to the nominal size of the deposit while the purchasing power of the latter is increased relative to the nominal size of the loan.

This transfer modifies the monetary impact on each of them, and the effect is cumulative. Assume in the above example that the money supply consists entirely of $100 nominal one-year deposits matched with $100 nominal one-year loans. If in any given year the money supply (loans and deposits) is increased by $20, or 20 percent, the impact on deposits and loans is very different. In effect, the real value of deposits will have risen that year by only $2 (with $18 effectively transferred to borrowers), while the value of loans will have increased by $38. An increase in nominal money of 20 percent, in other words, is associated with a 2 percent real increase in deposits and a 38 percent real increase in loans.

This is what it means to say that financial repression creates a bifurcation of monetary growth. For households, and net depositors more generally, real monetary expansion is in effect much lower than nominal monetary expansion because of the implicit financial repression "tax." As a consequence, consumption growth and consumer price inflation will seem abnormally low. For manufacturers, real estate developers, infrastructure investors, and other net borrowers, real monetary expansion is in effect much greater than nominal monetary expansion because of an implicit financial repression "subsidy," and so asset inflation and capacity growth seem abnormally high.

Perhaps one way of thinking about it is to consider how to make a comparable impact in a market system. Imagine if somehow the United States were to enact a law whose result was that every time the Fed expanded the money supply, a one-off tax was imposed on households, the proceeds of which were transferred to corporate borrowers. If that happened, monetary expansion would be much less likely to cause an increase in demand for consumer products (and so would create much less consumer price inflation) and much more likely to cause a surge in production.

This effective "tax" suggests that in a financially repressed system, it is normal that the impact of nominal monetary expansion will seem much greater in one sector of the economy than in another, with the difference reflecting the net lending or net borrowing position of that sector. The impact of monetary expansion on the behavior of the saver is much lower than it is in a market-based financial system, all other things being the same. The impact on the behavior of the borrower, meanwhile, is much higher than it is in a market-based financial system, all other things being the same.

Under these conditions it is not surprising that the economy can seem to be operating under conflicting monetary systems. Consumption behaves as it would in an economy with much lower monetary growth, and production and asset prices behave as they would in an economy with much higher monetary growth.

I will leave it to an ambitious doctoral student to work out the full monetary implications of financial repression and to formalize a model of monetary growth under financial repression. But it is worth noting that there are several other real implications of this bifurcation in monetary policy, all of which apply to the Chinese economy:

a.) Financial repression creates in effect a two-speed economy. There will normally be a growing imbalance between the net saving and net borrowing sides of the economy, and the latter should grow much more quickly than the former.

b.) By subsidizing the production side of the economy and penalizing the consumption side, financial repression must always force up the domestic savings rate. This may seem at first counterintuitive because we normally associate lower interest rates with lower savings, but it is an automatic consequence of the very different wealth effect that changes in interest rates have on market-based financial systems and financially repressed financial systems. Savings, after all, are simply the difference between consumption and production, and any process that forces production to grow more quickly than consumption automatically forces up the savings rate.

Financially repressed systems with artificially low interest rates tend historically to have much higher savings rates than market systems. They also have much higher savings rates than financial systems in which interest rates are abnormally high. But oddly enough, the higher savings rates are almost always ascribed to cultural preferences. Rather than explain differential savings rates by cultural factors, it seems far more promising to explain them as consequences of financial repression.

c.) To rebalance the two sides of the economy, policymakers must either eliminate, or even reverse, the transfer created by financial repression (that is, either nominal interest rates must rise or GDP growth must drop) or they must implement another mechanism that directly transfers wealth from net borrowers to net lenders.

d.) The more interest rates are repressed, the harder it is for consumption growth to keep up with production growth because monetary policy driving consumption is effectively much "tighter" than monetary policy driving production.

e.) Consumer price inflation is not the appropriate measure by which to gauge domestic monetary conditions.

f.) Increases and reductions in interest rates are not expansionary or contractionary in the way we might expect in an open financial system. An increase in interest rates may act to contract investment, but contrary to conventional wisdom it actually expands consumption because it reduces the wealth transfer from the saver to the borrower. This allows the saver to increase consumption.

g.) For the same reason, consumer price inflation in a financially repressed system can be self-correcting. If inflation rises but interest rates do not, the bifurcation of monetary growth will increase because the difference between the "correct" interest rate and the nominal rate increases. In that case any given nominal monetary expansion is accompanied by an even lower (or negative) real expansion from the point of view of consumers as net savers. By lowering the real cost of credit for borrowers, it can expand production. Increasing production while reducing consumption, of course, puts downward pressure on prices.

h.) Monetary expansion accelerates investment and asset price inflation. If inflation rises but interest rates do not, any given nominal monetary expansion is accompanied by an even greater real expansion for net borrowers.

i.) This may be why in financially repressed economies, regulators often resort to formal or informal loan quotas. Without loan quotas, monetary expansion for borrowers may far exceed the needs of the economy, even as monetary expansion for depositors is too tight.

j.) As long as the rest of the world can accommodate the consequent excess of production over consumption, the bifurcation in monetary policy will not seem to be a problem. Once the world cannot accommodate it, however, the bifurcation of monetary expansion will create deflationary pressures.

k.) As long as the rapid increase in monetary expansion for borrowers does not result in a misallocation of capital, the bifurcation in monetary policy will not seem to be a problem. But once rapid money expansion leads to increasingly wasted investment—as it eventually always must—the bifurcation of monetary expansion will create asset inflation and an unsustainable increase in debt (because debt rises faster than debt-servicing capacity).

l.) Deflation or disinflation partially or wholly resolves the bifurcation by forcing real interest rates toward their "correct" level (because real deposit and lending rates rise in a deflationary environment if there is no change in the nominal interest rate). Under deflation, we would expect to see a narrowing, or even a reversal, of the gap between consumption growth and GDP growth.

m.) Slower GDP growth partially or wholly resolves the bifurcation by forcing real interest rates toward their "correct" level (in a market system, nominal interest rates move naturally in line with nominal GDP growth). Under conditions of much slower GDP growth, we would expect to see a narrowing, or even a reversal, of the gap between consumption growth and GDP growth. This, for example, is what happened in Japan after 1990.

n.) Disintermediation of the banking system, to the extent that it reduces the impact of financial repression, may create an unexpected burst in consumer price inflation. This is less true to the extent that, like in China, disintermediation is limited to the rich, since the consumption impact of higher income on the rich is limited.

ASSET PRICE INFLATION

To summarize, in a financially repressed system in which consumers tend to be net savers and producers net borrowers, consumers and producers experience very different monetary impacts of the same underlying monetary conditions. Producers exist in an environment in which the impact of monetary growth is much faster than for consumers.

There are two problems, then, that must arise when a financially repressed system experiences long periods of rapid money growth. First, as growth in production systematically exceeds growth in consumption, absent exponential growth in investment, a growing trade surplus is necessary to resolve the growing imbalance. Once there are constraints on the ability of the trade surplus to continue growing—for example, the global financial crisis has caused a collapse in the ability of the rest of the world to absorb China's rising trade surplus—the only way to prevent a collapse in growth is to increase investment even more.

But if investment is being misallocated, the second problem is simply exacerbated. Rapid monetary expansion, exacerbated by the bifurcation created by financial repression, has a tendency to result in capital misallocation and asset price inflation because it accelerates monetary growth. If the response by policymakers to a contraction in the world's ability to absorb rising trade surpluses is to engineer a further increase in investment, we would expect debt to surge and more investment to be wasted. In short, debt will become unsustainable much more quickly.

This seems to be exactly what happened in China during the 2008–2009 global crisis. Before the crisis, debt was already rising at an unsustainable pace, thanks to many years of the combination of rapid monetary growth and monetary policy bifurcation. China's trade surplus also soared as production was forced to rise much more quickly than consumption.

The crisis caused a collapse in China's trade surplus. In order to limit the impact on Chinese growth, Beijing engineered an extraordinary increase in domestic investment. What is more, Beijing increased both the total amount of loans and deposits outstanding while lowering the real interest rate even further. The net impact was to increase the financial repression tax on households—a tax that went directly to subsidizing borrowers.

This certainly resolved the problem of a sharp decline in growth caused by a collapse in the trade surplus. But it did so by exacerbating the investment bubble and accelerating the rate at which the growth in debt exceeded the growth in debt-servicing capacity. It also worsened the consumption imbalance. It is probably not a coincidence that it was only in 2010 that most analysts belatedly recognized the impact of soaring debt in China on the surge in local and municipal debt. This realization probably came at the instigation of a report by Victor Shih, then a professor of political economy at Northwestern University and until then one of only a handful of skeptics of China's "miracle" growth model.[3]

As Chinese growth rates stayed high even in the midst of the worst global economy in seventy years—a fact that was a necessary consequence of the combination of increasing financial repression and a surge in monetary growth—there were always likely to be two factors that would undermine growth: first, if the pace of monetary expansion slowed, and second, if the financial repression tax declined.

What does it mean to say that the financial repression tax declines? This doesn't simply mean that interest rates rise, but rather that interest rates rise relative to GDP growth. In a market-based system, over long periods of time nominal interest rates are broadly in line with nominal GDP growth rates. This means that savers and borrowers fairly distribute the returns on growth in proportion to the amount of risk they take. Of course, if interest rates are artificially low, savers receive a disproportionately lower share of the benefits of growth and investors a disproportionately higher share.

The greater the difference between nominal lending rates and the nominal GDP growth rate, the greater the financial repression tax. In China during the first decade of this century, nominal GDP growth rates were 12–16 percent, depending on which period you measure and what assumptions you make about GDP growth. During the same period, nominal interest rates have been roughly 6–7 percent. This gives some idea of the extent of the financial repression tax, although even this example understates its extent because the spread between the lending rate

---

3 Victor Shih, "China's Stimulus Creates Non-Performing Loans," *Wall Street Journal*, February 8, 2010.

and the deposit rate is set artificially high, thus lowering even more the returns to depositors (an additional tax is effectively levied on depositors to recapitalize the banks).

The important point is that beginning sometime in late 2011, both conditions were in place. As debt continued to rise in China and as slowing growth eroded the trade surplus, there is evidence that beginning in 2010 capital flight from China began to surge. Meanwhile, beginning sometime in the fourth quarter of 2011, speculative inflows into the renminbi began drying up. The combination turned China's position from running net capital inflows to running net capital outflows (excluding changes in central bank reserves, which by definition balance out total flows to zero).

As a result, in late 2011 and 2012 we witnessed for the first time China's reserves rise by less than the already-much-lower current account surplus. By the middle of 2012, net capital outflows actually exceeded the current account surplus (reserves, in other words, declined in spite of a current account surplus).

As Chinese money creation slowed, exacerbated by monetary bifurcation, Chinese growth slowed along with it. This had the impact of reducing the financial repression tax (the difference between nominal GDP growth and nominal interest rates narrowed). The consequence was predictable: GDP growth slowed far more quickly in 2012 than even the pessimists had expected.

This is part of the self-reinforcing tendencies that financial repression creates for an economy. Rapid growth increases the financial repression tax, which tends to create even more rapid growth by reducing the real cost of capital. Slowing growth reduces the financial repression tax, which slows growth even further. These self-reinforcing tendencies embedded in the national capital structure are typical of developing countries and one of their great sources of economic volatility—one that tends to undermine long-term growth.[4]

---

4 For more on self-reinforcing tendencies in developing country capital structures and how they reduce long-term growth prospects, see Michael Pettis, *The Volatility Machine: Emerging Economies and the Threat of Financial Collapse* (New York: Oxford University Press, 2001).

CHAPTER 5

HOW WILL CHINA REBALANCE?

We need to keep the impact of financial repression in mind in understanding the Chinese growth model. It is a fundamental cause of China's rapid growth in economic activity and its extraordinary imbalances. To return to the narrative of chapters 2 and 3, the key vulnerability of my argument that China has no choice but to rebalance its economy within two to three years, and an argument that hinges on understanding the role of financial repression, is whether or not we believe that investment in the aggregate is being misallocated in China and, if so, whether this has been true for very long.

In chapter 3 I argued that there are very strong conceptual reasons for assuming a powerful tendency within China to misallocate investment. This was always likely to be one of the automatic consequences of China's repressed financial system, which after so many years of delivering robust growth had shifted toward delivering growth driven by capital misallocation. Under these conditions, in which the state has unrestricted access to national savings and few constraints on how they are allocated, no economic system in history has failed to experience capital misallocation. Not to see the same in China would be an astonishing new development in economic history.

But there are additional reasons for believing that capital has been massively misallocated in China. Of course, capital misallocation can never be proven until well after the fact, especially when capital is spent on large-scale infrastructure projects, whose ultimate value is very sensitive to assumptions about future growth. But if capital had been misallocated on a significant scale in China during the past several years, we would expect to see certain kinds of circumstantial evidence.

- If capital is being misallocated because interest rates are too low, then it is reasonable to assume that this would occur both in areas where we can measure misallocation and in areas where we cannot. Are there areas where we can measure it? It turns out that in fact there are: state-owned enterprises, like other large-scale investors, have benefited from artificially low interest rates, and it is quite easy to prove that over the past decade they have been value destroyers on a very significant scale.

  Studies done by the mainland think tank Unirule Institute of Economics suggest that well over 100 percent, and perhaps much closer to 200 percent, of the aggregate profitability of state-owned enterprises in China over the past decade can be explained by monopoly pricing and direct subsidies. Without these subsidies, according to the study, state-owned enterprises earned a negative return on equity equal to 6 to 7 percent.[1]

  It should be noted that both monopoly pricing and direct subsidies represent transfers from the household sector to subsidize economic activity. Monopoly pricing occurs through the higher prices charged to consumers. Direct subsidies occur in a variety of ways depending on the subsidy. Subsidized land and energy prices, for example, are paid for either by various forms of taxation or by government borrowing at financially repressed rates, which effectively shifts the costs to households in the form of repressed deposit rates.

  More important than monopoly pricing and direct subsidies are the indirect subsidies. The most important of these is the repressed borrowing cost (an undervalued currency is also a subsidy paid for indirectly by households, in the form of an effective consumption tax on imported goods). The interest rate subsidy is very high relative to the profitability of the large borrowers.

---

1   "The Nature, Performance and Reform of State-Owned Enterprises," Unirule Institute of Economics, 2011.

A 2009 study done by the think tank associated with the Hong Kong Monetary Authority found that the aggregate profitability of China's entire state-owned enterprise sector over the decade could be explained by the roughly 1 percentage point reduction in borrowing costs caused by implicit state guarantees.[2] Because the artificial reduction in interest rates reduces the real interest rate by anywhere from 5 to 10 percentage points, depending on the assumption you use, it follows that artificially low interest rates may explain anywhere from 500 to 1,000 percent of the aggregate profitability of the state-owned sector.

From these studies it is pretty clear that judged purely on an economic basis, the state-owned sector is a large-scale destroyer of value (in the aggregate—some companies, of course, are not), and these companies are able to show substantial profits only because of very large, and mostly hidden, subsidies. This, of course, does not prove that capital in China has been misallocated in the aggregate. The fact that real returns have been significantly negative in one of the few areas in which it is possible to measure returns, however, suggests that at the very least the financial system has the capacity to fund non-economic investment very easily.

• If debt-funded capital is being misallocated, debt must be rising faster than debt-servicing capacity. If this is the case, at least two consequences should be apparent. First, we should see evidence that debt is rising too quickly and at some point is beginning to cause strains in the banking system. Second, if debt has been rising faster than debt-servicing capacity, either the borrowing entity must have defaulted at some point or there must have been a transfer of resources from another part of the economy in order to service the debt.

To address the first, there is no way of measuring precisely the relation between growth in debt and growth in debt-servicing capacity, especially when accurate debt numbers are extremely hard to obtain in China. But perhaps it is sufficient simply

---

2 Giovanni Ferri and Li-Gang Liu, "Honor Thy Creditors Before Thy Shareholders: Are the Profits of Chinese State-Owned Enterprises Real?" Hong Kong Institute for Monetary Research, Working Paper 16, 2009.

to follow the debate about the banking system, especially in the past two years, to get a sense of how rapidly debt has been rising. I will not summarize this debate since it is extensive and easy to observe (for example, the excellent Chinese weekly *Caixin* has widely documented the rapidly rising bank loans, receivables, informal debt, off-balance-sheet instruments, and so on), but it is pretty clear that there are grounds to worry that debt has emerged as a substantial problem in China. Statements and actions from a wide range of policymakers, including regulators and prominent bankers like Xiao Gang (chairman of the Bank of China) suggest that, at the very least, they are concerned about rising debt.

A wide variety of private-sector estimates about the true level of government debt, including contingent liabilities through the banking system, reinforce this concern. They place total debt at anywhere from 80 to 120 percent of GDP, and these estimates usually do not include possible bad debt rising on the balance sheets of state-owned enterprises (where receivables have soared in recent years) or in the informal banking market. In addition, these estimates ignore the net indebtedness of the central bank, whose mismatched balance sheet (foreign currency assets equivalent to roughly 50 percent of GDP are funded by renminbi liabilities) causes net indebtedness to rise directly as a function of the roughly 30 percent appreciation in the currency since July 2005.

• The second consequence is more revealing. Because there have been few major defaults in China, clearly if capital were being misallocated there must have been a transfer of resources from another part of the economy in order to service the difference between debt and debt-servicing capacity. Identifying the sector of the economy that has paid for the transfer of resources would provide strong circumstantial evidence that capital has indeed been misallocated.

It turns out that it is relatively easy to identify the sector that has paid for the difference between the real debt-servicing cost and debt-servicing capacity. This sector is, as it nearly always is in any economy, the household sector. China's household sector has paid for the bad debt in two ways. First, and most obviously, the wide spread between the deposit and lending rates mandated by the central bank had the effect of guaranteeing substantial profits to the banking sector. These profits allowed the banks to absorb nonperforming loans, but, of course, this came at the expense of the household sector.

More importantly, by artificially reducing interest rates to well below the nominal GDP growth rate, and even to negative real rates, the central bank effectively granted significant debt forgiveness to borrowers every year over the past decade. An insolvent borrower, after all, can easily continue to service his debt if the coupon is set low enough and the principal is constantly rolled over, both of which are the case in China.

After many years, the hidden debt forgiveness created by artificially low coupons can make it seem as if the borrower simply "grew" his way back into solvency. But the borrower seemed to do so because the household sector, in the form of deposits earning too-low returns, granted hidden debt forgiveness.

We know that the household sector paid for all these bad loans because after twenty years of rapidly rising GDP and rapidly rising household income, China began the last decade with a very low household income share of GDP. At 46 percent of GDP in 2000, this level of consumption was not unprecedented, but it was likely to occur only in the case of large economies that had suffered crises. And normally, after such low household consumption amid such rapid growth for so many years, we would have expected some catching up of the household income share.

How would this catching up take place? As China continued investing at a furious pace, if investment had indeed been value creating in the aggregate, the value creation of some of the earlier investment should have begun to accrue to the benefit of the household sector. Some investments, of course, may prove beneficial only over the long term, but once they begin to generate productivity growth that exceeds the cost of the investment, it is natural that at least part of this productivity growth accrues to the workers who created the value.

But Chinese workers did not begin to see the consequences of earlier investment show up as a higher share of total wealth for them; on the contrary, their share of wealth continued declining, and more rapidly than ever after 2000. We know this because from 2000 to 2010, household consumption dropped from 46 percent of GDP, which is already a very low share, to an astonishingly low 34 percent of GDP. The collapse in the household share of China's GDP, in other words, occurred because households had been forced to pay for the difference between the real debt-servicing cost of a decade of misallocated investment and the debt-servicing capacity created by that investment.

If this was not the reason, the only other plausible explanation is that the vast bulk of Chinese investment from the late 1970s onward was in projects whose real payoff was not likely to occur for many decades from the date of the investment. Could this be true? Perhaps, if the investment were in schooling for very young children, or in extremely advanced technology (although such a long payoff for investment in the aggregate would have been historically unprecedented).

But, in fact, Chinese investors, as in other developing countries, tend to have short-term horizons, and most Chinese investment seems to have been in the kind of investment typical for poor countries. It went into increasing manufacturing capacity, real estate development, and transportation infrastructure projects. This kind of investment typically has much shorter payoff horizons than implied by nearly thirty-five years of decline in the household consumption share of GDP. In fact rapid depreciation is a special concern in China given the very low quality of construction and materials.

THE IMF WEIGHS IN

On that very subject, the IMF published a very interesting and widely noticed study in late 2012 in which the authors, Il Houng Lee, Murtaza Syed, and Liu Xueyan, argued that there is strong evidence that China is significantly overinvesting.[3] According to the abstract:

---

3   Il Houng Lee, Murtaza Syed, and Liu Xueyan, "Is China Over-Investing and Does It Matter?" IMF Working Paper 12/277, November 2012.

Now close to 50 percent of GDP, this paper assesses the appropriateness of China's current investment levels. It finds that China's capital-to-output ratio is within the range of other emerging markets, but its economic growth rates stand out, partly due to a surge in investment over the last decade. Moreover, its investment is significantly higher than suggested by cross-country panel estimation.

This deviation has been accumulating over the last decade, and at nearly 10 percent of GDP is now larger and more persistent than experienced by other Asian economies leading up to the Asian crisis. However, because its investment is predominantly financed by domestic savings, a crisis appears unlikely when assessed against dependency on external funding. But this does not mean that the cost is absent. Rather, it is distributed to other sectors of the economy through a hidden transfer of resources, estimated at an average of 4 percent of GDP per year.

The study makes a very strong case in favor of the overinvestment claim. China's investment rate is so high, the skeptics have argued for many years, that even ignoring the tremendous evidence of misallocated investment, unless Beijing has uncovered a secret formula that allows it (and the tens of thousands of minor government officials and heads of state-owned enterprises who can unleash investment without much oversight) to consistently identify high-quality investment in a way that no other country in history has been able, there is likely to be a systematic tendency to wasted investment.

This seems to be confirmed by the IMF study. Interestingly enough, while two of the authors of the study work for the IMF, Liu Xueyan, the third, is a senior fellow in the Institute of Economic Research at the National Development and Reform Commission of China. We should be careful about how much to read into this, but it is worth noting that both the World Bank report in April 2012 and this IMF study have involved input from important mainland think tanks.[4]

This is noteworthy because both documents have come out strongly in the direction that the China "skeptics" had been arguing for many

---

4   World Bank, Beijing, "China Quarterly Update: Sustaining Growth," World Bank, April 2012.

years. They identify the urgent need for adjustment and suggest—very delicately—how politically difficult it would be to implement the necessary adjustments. This seems to be part of the tough debate that is taking place within Beijing policymaking circles over the need to implement the political reforms that would be a necessary part of the economic rebalancing, and I assume the reformers are eager to recruit the World Bank and the IMF to their points of view.

One of the implications of the IMF study is that households and small and medium-size enterprises have been forced to subsidize growth at a cost to them of well over 4 percent of GDP annually. My own back-of-the-envelope calculations suggest that the cost to households is actually 5–8 percent of GDP—perhaps because I also include the implicit subsidy to recapitalize the banks in the form of the excess spread between the lending and deposit rates—but certainly we agree that this has been a massive transfer to subsidize growth.

This subsidy also explains most of the collapse in the household share of China's GDP over the past twelve years. With household income only 50 percent of GDP, a transfer every year of 4 percent of GDP, let alone 5–8 percent, requires ferocious growth in household income for it just to keep pace with GDP, something it has never done until, possibly, 2012.

The size of the hidden transfer from the household sector makes it very clear that short of eliminating this subsidy—which basically means abandoning the growth model—it would be almost impossible to get the household and consumption shares of GDP to rise and still maintain China's high GDP growth. The transfer of wealth from the household sector to maintain high levels of investment is simply too great, and this will be made all the more clear as the growth impact per unit of investment declines.

Another implication of the IMF study is that for China to line up with other equivalent countries at this stage of its economic takeoff, Beijing would have to reduce the investment share of GDP by at least 10 percentage points and perhaps as much as 20 percentage points. Aside from pointing out that the sectors of the economy that have benefited from such extraordinarily high investment are unlikely to celebrate such a finding, I have three comments. First, after many years in which China has invested far more than other countries at its stage of development, one could presumably argue that in order to get back to the "correct" ratio, investment should be lower than the peer group, not equal to the peer group. In that case investment has to drop by a lot more than 10 percentage points.

After all, if China's deviation from the experience of other countries is meaningful, then after a few years of substantial deviation, it cannot be enough for China simply to return to the mean. It must come in lower than the mean for many years so that on average the deviation is eliminated.

Second, even if China had kept investment at the "correct" level, as measured by the peer group, this would not imply that China had not overinvested. A very quick glance at the countries included in the peer group analysis, which the study lists, suggests that many of these countries, after years of very high investment, themselves experienced deep crises or lost decades.

This implies that these countries themselves may have overinvested, and so even if Chinese investment levels were not much higher than that of the peer group (and it was mainly in the past decade that Chinese investment rose to much higher levels—not in the 1990s, exactly as the skeptics, using more qualitative measures, had been suggesting), this could nonetheless be worrying. China would still have a difficult adjustment for the same reasons that many if not most of the peer group countries had difficult adjustments.

The average number driven by the peer group sample, in other words, is not in itself an "optimal" level of investment. It might already be too high. That Chinese investment levels are 25 percent higher than theirs as a share of GDP is all the more worrying.

The third point is more technical. If Chinese investment levels are much higher than optimal (assuming the peer group average is indeed optimal), of course the best solution for China is immediately to reduce investment until it reaches the right level. The longer investment rates are too high, the greater the impact of losses that eventually have to be amortized, and the worse off China is likely to be.

But it will be exceedingly hard for China very quickly to bring investment down by 10 full percentage points as a share of GDP. Let us assume instead that China has five years to bring investment levels down to the "correct" level, and let us assume further that the "correct" level is indeed 10 percentage points below where it is today. Both assumptions are, I think, dangerous because I am not convinced that an investment level of 40 percent of GDP is the "correct" level for China—I think it must be much lower. Nor do I think China has five years to make the necessary adjustment without running a serious risk of a financial crisis.

But let us ignore both objections and give China five years to bring investment down to 40 percent of GDP from its current level of 50 percent. Clearly Chinese investment must grow more slowly than GDP for this to happen. How much more slowly? The arithmetic is simple. It depends on what we assume GDP growth will be over the next five years, but investment has to grow by roughly at least 4.5 percentage points less than GDP for this condition to be met.

If Chinese GDP grows at 7 percent, in other words, Chinese investment must grow at 2.3 percent. If China grows at 5 percent, investment must grow at 0.4 percent. And if China grows at 3 percent, which is much closer to my ten-year view, investment growth must actually contract by 1.5 percent. Only in this way can investment drop by 10 percentage points as a share of GDP in the next five years.

The conclusion should be obvious. Any meaningful rebalancing in China's extraordinary rate of overinvestment is consistent only with a very sharp reduction in the growth rate of investment, and perhaps even a contraction in investment growth. If this contraction in investment growth itself pushes down the growth rate of household income, it will have to drop even further for the economy to rebalance.

In fact, over the next few years China will indeed undergo a sharp contraction in investment growth, I believe, but my point here is not to predict the actual growth rate of investment but simply to suggest that even under the most optimistic of scenarios it will be very hard to keep investment growth high. Either Beijing moves quickly to bring investment growth down sharply, or overinvestment will contribute to further financial fragility, leading ultimately to the point where credit cannot expand quickly enough and investment will collapse anyway. This is just arithmetic.

THE REBALANCE SCENARIOS

The extent of Chinese overinvestment—even if we assume that it has not already caused significant fragility in the banking system and enormous hidden losses yet to be amortized—requires a very sharp contraction just to get back to a "normal" that, in the past, was anyway associated with difficult economic adjustments. It is hard to imagine how such a sharp contraction in investment will itself not lead to a sharp drop in GDP growth, and the IMF paper recognizes this:

> To the extent that elevated levels of investment during the post-crisis period in China were somehow abnormal and necessitated by the sharp external slowdown, the challenge now is how to return to a more "normal" level of investment without compromising growth and macroeconomic stability.

As studies like this one, and many others, make evident what the historical precedents suggested would happen—that China would overinvest and eventually be forced to address the balance sheet implications of this overinvestment—it is important to consider the ways in which China can most easily, or least painfully, absorb the costs and adjust its economy. Once we accept that investment is being significantly misallocated and that the current system cannot resolve the problem, we must agree that consumption will become a greater share of GDP over the next five to ten years. What's more, we must agree that the only way to increase the consumption share of GDP is to increase the household income (or wealth) share of GDP.[5]

China, in other words, must stop transferring income from households to the state and in fact must reverse those transfers. As Chinese household income and wealth become a greater share of the overall economy, so will Chinese consumption. The key is that after three decades during which household income declined as a share of the economic pie (and the state

---

5   Technically there is another way, and that is for household debt to surge as households borrow to fund consumption. But most evidence suggests that consumer financing is correlated with household wealth, and anyway China will require many years to develop a robust consumer-financing infrastructure.

sector, which many think of as a proxy for the wealth of the political elite, increased its share), China must now engineer a development model in which household income rises as a share of the economic pie.

Although difficult, transferring wealth from the state to the household sector is not impossible. As I see it, the various ways in which this transfer can take place can be accounted for by one or more of the six following scenarios:

1. Beijing can continue with its existing growth model, maintaining its high investment growth rates, until it reaches its debt capacity limits, after which a sudden stop in investment will force up the household share (albeit under conditions of negative growth).

2. Beijing can quickly reverse the transfers that created the imbalances by, for example, raising real interest rates sharply, forcing up the foreign exchange value of the currency by 10 to 20 percent overnight, and pushing up wages, or by lowering income and consumption taxes.

3. Beijing can slowly reverse the transfers in the same way.

4. Beijing can directly transfer wealth from the state sector to the private sector by privatizing assets and using the proceeds directly or indirectly to boost household wealth.

5. Beijing can indirectly transfer wealth from the state sector to the private sector by absorbing private-sector debt.

6. Beijing can cut investment sharply, resulting in a collapse in growth, but it can mitigate the employment impact of this collapse by hiring unemployed workers for various make-work programs and paying their salaries out of state resources.

Notice that all of these options effectively have China doing the same thing: in each case, the state share of GDP is reduced and the household share is increased. There are, however, very big differences in how the changes are distributed among various parts of the household and state sectors.

Notice also that the changing share of GDP reveals little or nothing about the actual GDP growth rate, or about the growth rate of either household wealth or state wealth. It just tells us something very important about relative growth rates.

For example, we can posit a case in which GDP grows by 9 percent annually while household income grows by 12–13 percent annually. In that case the rest of the economy would grow by roughly 5–6 percent annually (household income is approximately half of GDP), and the distribution of this growth would be shared between the state and business sectors. This might be considered an example of a "good case" scenario of rebalancing.

Alternatively, we can posit that annual GDP growth is 0 percent. In that case the annual growth in household income might be 3–4 percent while the state and business sectors contract at roughly 3–4 percent. This would be an example of a "bad case" scenario. Of course, we can posit an even worse case, in which GDP contracts by 3 percent while household consumption is flat and the state and business sectors contract at roughly 6–7 percent.

THE POLITICAL ECONOMY OF REBALANCING

It is worth making three points about these different scenarios. First, in any of these cases China rebalances, but the way in which it rebalances will have very different growth implications. Second, notice that even in the bad cases, household income growth can be quite robust, which means that fears of social instability as Chinese growth slows are exaggerated. If a Chinese growth slowdown occurs with real rebalancing, household income can continue to rise quickly. Because rebalancing implies an asymmetry in growth rates of the different sectors—more specifically a reversal of the process by which household income growth lags behind GDP growth to one in which it leads GDP growth—slower GDP growth does not mean symmetrically slower growth across the board.

But—and this is the third point—this is not the only consequence of the asymmetry. The real cost of the rebalancing, it turns out, falls on the state sector, and we will have to keep this in mind as we consider the choices that Beijing must make. "There are two things that are important in politics," as Republican political operative Mark Hanna reminisced in 1895. "The first is money, and I can't remember what the second one is."

I am not sure what the second one is either, but for the past twenty years, and especially the past ten, the state and business share of a rapidly growing economic pie was also growing, which meant extraordinary growth in the value of assets controlled by the state sector and the economic elite. The household share of the growing economic pie, of course, contracted, but the rapid growth in the pie ensured that household income grew quite rapidly nonetheless, even as the household share of total income declined.

When we reverse this process, as we must if there is to be rebalancing, any slowdown in GDP growth may be minimally felt by the household sector (if the rebalancing is managed in an orderly way), but even a scenario of very high GDP growth must result in much slower growth in the value of state-sector income and assets. Of course, if GDP growth actually slows sharply, which I expect it will, the growth in the value of state sector assets will drop even more sharply and perhaps even turn negative.

This is the fly in the ointment. The change in the growth rate of the state sector will almost certainly be at the heart of the political economy choices, and difficulties, that Beijing will be forced to address in the next few years. It was always likely to be much easier to keep political leaders and factions happy when the value of the state sector was growing comfortably in the double-digit range, as it has for much of the past decade when GDP grew in the low double digits. It is likely to be much more difficult as GDP growth slows and the state sector slows even more, growing in low single digits, or even contracting.

In fact, the real political difficulty of slower GDP growth as China rebalances is not necessarily a function of discontent at the household level. It is far more likely to be caused by discontent at the level of political elites. The adjustment from a rapidly growing China, with even more rapid growth in the value of assets controlled and exploited by the political elite, to a more slowly growing China, with slower or negative growth in the value of assets controlled and exploited by the political elite, is likely to be controversial and much resisted.

Minxin Pei, a professor of government at Claremont McKenna College, implicitly makes a similar argument.[6] In an article for Project Syndicate, he says:

> When sound economic advice is divorced from political reality, it probably will not be very useful advice. The history of multilateral financial institutions like the International Monetary Fund and the World Bank is littered with well-intentioned and technically feasible economic policy prescriptions that political leaders ignored. But that has not stopped these institutions from trying.
>
> The latest attempt is the World Bank's just-released and much-applauded report *China 2030: Building a Modern, Harmonious, and Creative High-Income Society*. As far as technical economic advice goes, the report is hard to top. It provides a detailed, thoughtful, and honest diagnosis of the Chinese economy's structural and institutional flaws, and calls for coherent and bold reforms to remove these fundamental obstacles to sustainable growth.
>
> Unfortunately, while the Bank's report has laid out a clear economic course that Chinese leaders should pursue for the sake of China, the Bank has shied away from the most critical question: Will the Chinese government actually heed its advice and swallow the bitter medicine, given the country's one-party political system?

Pei argues that serious political constraints inhibit Beijing's ability to force the necessary reforms recommended by the World Bank. For example, when it comes to reducing the power of inefficient and wasteful state-owned enterprises:

> There is little doubt that reducing the SOEs' power would make the Chinese economy far more efficient and dynamic. But it is hard to imagine that a one-party regime would be willing to destroy its political base.

---

6 Minxin Pei, "China's Politics of the Economically Possible," Project Syndicate, March 16, 2012.

In a sense Pei makes the same argument I do, but from a different angle. I argue that you can discuss as much as you like what Beijing proclaims it will do, but what it actually does will necessarily be constrained by what is *economically* possible. Pei says you can talk all you want about what economic policies Beijing will follow, but what it actually does will necessarily be constrained by what is *politically* possible. If you were to superimpose Pei's political constraints on top of my economic constraints, you would presumably be left with a much more accurate measure of what can actually happen.

I leave the politics of economic decisionmaking to Minxin Pei and other politically savvy analysts, like Victor Shih of UC San Diego, but in thinking about economic constraints it might be useful to examine each of the six options I have listed above.[7] This allows us to see what the consequences for growth each of the options might involve, as well as what disadvantages they have and how they would play out.

CAN CHINA INCREASE EXPORT COMPETITIVENESS?

Before we discuss, in the next two chapters, the risks, challenges, and implications associated with each of the paths open to China, it may help in understanding the process to consider what rebalancing means to such widely discussed issues as China's currency regime.

From July 2005 to February 2012, the renminbi rose by just over 30 percent in nominal U.S. dollars. Although on a trade-weighted basis, adjusted for changes in relative productivity growth, the revaluation has been much less than 30 percent, the increase in the value of the renminbi has nonetheless been seen, correctly, as a part of China's rebalancing process.

But after rising for nearly seven years, the renminbi dropped 1 percent against the dollar between February and September 2012 before appreciating again. Not surprisingly, this long period of depreciation set off intense speculation about Beijing's trade intentions. The threat of a weaker

---

7 See especially Victor Shih, *Factions and Finance in China: Elite Conflict and Inflation* (New York: Cambridge University Press, 2009).

renminbi making Chinese exports more competitive abroad and foreign imports more expensive in China raised worries in a world already struggling with weak demand growth. It still does.

But these worries may have been unfounded. If China is serious about rebalancing its economy, devaluing the renminbi will not result in a net improvement in export competitiveness. China's export competitiveness will deteriorate no matter what Beijing does to the currency.

To understand why, it is important to see that as part of its rebalancing, and as we have discussed many times in this book, China must sharply reduce investment, or at least reduce the growth rate of investment. In principle the adverse impact of slower growth in investment should be offset by faster growth in consumption, but it has proven very difficult for China to raise the GDP share of consumption, largely because consumption-constraining policies are at the heart of China's growth model and indeed at the heart of investment growth models more generally. It will take many years of adjustment before consumption is large enough and can grow into its proper role.

This means that during the adjustment process, it is a virtual certainty that growth in China will slow significantly for many years. That's because if Beijing brings investment growth down more quickly than can be counterbalanced by an increase in consumption growth, its overall growth rate must slow sharply. This is true almost by definition.

I say "almost" because there is a third source of demand that affects domestic growth—the trade surplus—and this is why there is now so much focus on the value of the renminbi. If China's trade surplus rises sharply during the adjustment process, overall economic growth rates could be much better than expected.

If the trade surplus contracts, however, growth will be worse. Clearly a healthy trade account would make it easier for Beijing to manage the adjustment process. For this reason many analysts, both foreign and Chinese, argue that by boosting China's competitiveness abroad, a weaker renminbi would provide some relief from the sharp expected slowdown associated with rebalancing.

But they are wrong. If China's trade balance improves because of a surge in foreign demand (pretty unlikely, given the state of the global economy), this would almost certainly be good for the economy and would allow the rebalancing process to be less painful. But if Beijing takes steps to increase China's competiveness abroad by artificially lowering costs domestically, including by depreciating the renminbi, it would have no effect on overall growth for any given level of economic rebalancing.

Why not? Because there is a lot more to Chinese competitiveness than the undervalued exchange rate. There are in fact three main mechanisms that explain the relatively low price of Chinese exports abroad, all of which transfer income from Chinese households to subsidize Chinese producers, albeit in very different ways. We have already discussed these three.

THE SOURCES OF CHINA'S EXPORT COMPETITIVENESS

The currency regime is certainly one of them, and the mechanism is fairly easy to understand. An undervalued currency spurs export competitiveness by subsidizing the local cost component for manufacturers. These implicit subsidies are effectively paid for by Chinese households in the form of artificially high prices for imported goods. Because all households, except perhaps subsistence farmers, are effectively net importers, an undervalued currency is a kind of consumption tax that effectively reduces the real value of their income.

The second mechanism, the difference between wage and productivity growth, does the same thing but with a different set of winners and losers. Chinese workers' wages have grown more slowly than productivity for all but the last two years of the past three decades, which means that until two years ago workers have received a steadily declining share of what they produce. Manufacturers and other employers benefit from this process because their wage payments are effectively subsidized, so the more labor-intensive production is, the greater the subsidy they implicitly receive.

The third mechanism, the most important, is artificially low interest rates. These reduce household income by reducing the return households receive on bank deposits; because of legal constraints on investment alternatives, the bulk of savings in China is in the form of bank deposits. Artificially lowered interest rates, however, increase manufacturing competitiveness by lowering the cost of capital. Of course, the more capital-intensive a manufacturer is, the more it benefits.

All these subsidies goose economic growth by subsidizing producers, but they distribute the benefits in different ways. The greater the local production component, the higher the subsidy created by an undervalued currency. The more labor intensive the manufacturer, the greater the subsidy created by low wages. And, finally, the more capital intensive the producer, the more it benefits from artificially low interest rates.

The mechanisms also distribute the costs in different ways. An undervalued currency hurts households in proportion to the value of imports in their total consumption basket. Low wages hurt workers and farmers. Low interest rates hurt households in proportion to the amount of their savings as a share of income.

Because they boost economic growth at the expense of households, these three mechanisms cause the economy to grow much faster than household income. As explained in chapter 2, this is the root of China's unbalanced economy—household income has grown so much more slowly than the economy that household consumption over the past three decades has collapsed as a share of GDP.

Rebalancing in China means by definition, however, that the household consumption share of GDP must rise, and the only effective way to do this is by raising the household income share of GDP. Revaluing the currency is one way of doing so. It increases the real income of households by reducing the cost of imports, and it raises local production costs for manufacturers.

But revaluing the currency is not the only way. Raising Chinese wages increases household income, too, while increasing labor costs for manufacturers. Finally, allowing interest rates to rise benefits households by increasing the return on savings, and it raises costs for capital-intensive manufacturers.

DOMESTIC PRIORITIES

As China rebalances, by definition Chinese household income must rise as a share of total GDP. This is the important point that is often forgotten in the debate about Chinese competitiveness. In the aggregate, as China rebalances, the net impact of changes in all three mechanisms must result in reduced subsidies to Chinese manufacturers and so, at least initially, in reduced Chinese competiveness abroad.

If Beijing wants to rebalance, and it decides to devalue the renminbi anyway, that just means that Beijing must raise wages or interest rates all the more in order to force a real increase in the growth rate of household income. Any improvement in Chinese export competitiveness achieved by devaluing the renminbi, in other words, would be fully made up for by a deterioration in Chinese export competitiveness caused by rising wages or rising interest rates.

This is ultimately what rebalancing means in the Chinese context. One way or another as China rebalances, it will lose competiveness abroad because it must raise the cost of production in favor of household income. In exchange, however, China's domestic market will become a bigger source of demand as Chinese households benefit from rebalancing. Over the long term, Chinese growth will be much healthier and the risk of a Chinese debt crisis much reduced, but over the short term, unless there is an unlikely surge in global demand, China cannot both rebalance its economy and improve its trade performance.

How China rebalances, then, will mainly reflect domestic priorities and political maneuvering. Revaluing the currency would disproportionately help middle- and working-class urban households—for whom import costs tend to be important—and disproportionately hurt manufacturers whose production costs are primarily local, that is, most manufacturers that are not in the processing trade.

If, however, China chooses to raise wages, it would disproportionately help urban workers and farmers and disproportionately hurt labor-intensive manufacturers and businesses in the services sector, both of which tend to be small and medium-size enterprises. And, finally, if China raises interest rates, it would disproportionately help middle-class savers and disproportionately hurt large, capital-intensive manufacturers.

These three strategies, in other words, broadly have the same impact on trade competitiveness, although in each case the winners and losers within China would be different. This is why we should not be overly concerned with what happens just to the exchange value of the renminbi. As long as China genuinely rebalances its economy—a painful process no matter how Beijing chooses to manage it—Chinese export costs will rise and in the short term Chinese goods will be less competitive in the global markets. (As rising domestic costs force China to increase productivity and innovation, over the longer term Chinese goods will actually boost Chinese competitiveness.)

The path China chooses to follow should be seen by the world primarily as something that affects the way the costs and benefits of rebalancing are distributed domestically. For the sake of more sustainable and equitable long-term growth, and in the interests of economic efficiency, it is almost certainly much better for China and the world if Beijing raises interest rates than if it revalues the renminbi. Because raising interest rates is likely to be opposed by the very powerful groups that benefit from excessively cheap capital, however, Beijing may instead put more focus on raising wages, which comes mainly at the detriment of economically efficient but politically weak small and medium-size enterprises and service industries.

China urgently needs to rebalance its economy, but how it chooses to do so should not be constrained by too much focus on the value of the renminbi. The exchange rate is only one of the mechanisms—and not even the most important mechanism—that will determine the price of Chinese goods abroad. It is domestic politics that will determine the form in which the rebalancing takes place, and as long as rebalancing occurs, the world should not overly emphasize the role of the currency.

Do not expect, in other words, that China will steal export share from the rest of the world while rebalancing its economy by depreciating the renminbi. Increasing competiveness in export markets is not compatible with rebalancing. As China rebalances, it has no choice but to reduce its export competitiveness. Even devaluing the renminbi would not improve Chinese competitiveness abroad, because Beijing would have to raise wages or interest rates all the more. Doing so would simply shift the brunt of the export adjustment from one group within the country to another.

CHAPTER 6

THE MECHANICS OF
REBALANCING

I n chapter 5 I argued that if we accept the argument that China must,
and will, rebalance its economy by reducing its reliance on investment and increasing its reliance on consumption, and if we further
accept the claim that the main explanation for China's extraordinarily low
consumption share of GDP is the extremely low household income share
of GDP, then it follows that China can rebalance only by increasing the
household income share of GDP.

To put it another way, after thirty years in which the household share
of GDP has contracted and the state and corporate share has expanded—
although GDP has grown so quickly that household income nonetheless
grew rapidly during this period—we must now pass over to a period of at
least a decade or two during which the household income share of GDP
expands while the state and corporate shares contract. Because this must
certainly occur under conditions of much slower GDP growth, it means
that more than 100 percent of the reduction in GDP growth must be
borne by the state and corporate sectors.

This rapid reduction—or even outright contraction—in the growth
of the state and corporate sectors has very important and difficult political implications for Beijing, and these implications will be at the heart of
the political economy choices for years. It does mean, however, that the
household sector will bear less than its share of the contraction in growth,
which should relieve concerns that slower growth in China will necessarily be accompanied by popular discontent.

In fact, some commentators argue that there need be no contraction at all in the growth rate of household income. The growth in household income might even speed up, they contend. For example, in a November 2012 debate I had with Nick Lardy of the Peterson Institute for International Economics, he argued:

> Assuming there is a 7% cap on real consumption growth is problematic to say the least. To begin with real private consumption expanded by an average of almost 10% per year over the last decade, not "roughly 7%," and last year it rose by more than 11% in real terms. Importantly, while the growth of real investment has fallen below its decade average in the past two years the pace of real consumption growth has been above its decade average. This suggests the potential for more robust consumption expenditure to offset slowing investment growth is far from theoretical.[1]

Lardy may be right, of course, but I think it is hard to argue that consumption growth will accelerate even as GDP growth is slowing without specifying the mechanism that would force this (a surge in consumer credit? a large transfer of wealth from the state sector to the household sector?). Whether or not household income growth accelerates or slows down, as a matter almost of definition it must exceed GDP growth if China is to rebalance, and this requires either a reversal of the transfers that forced greater GDP growth at the expense of the household sector or some other mechanism that can cause a surge in household wealth. As I discussed in chapter 5, logically it seems that there are only six ways, broadly speaking, in which China can rebalance:

1. Beijing can do nothing, maintaining its high investment growth rates, until it reaches its debt capacity limits, after which a sudden stop in investment will force up the household share (albeit under conditions of negative growth).

2. Beijing can quickly reverse the transfers that created the imbalances by, for example, raising real interest rates sharply, forcing up the foreign exchange value of the currency by 10 to

1 "Lardy vs. Pettis: Debating China's Economic Future," China RealTime Report, *Wall Street Journal*, November 8, 2012.

20 percent overnight, and pushing up wages, or by lowering income and consumption taxes.

3. Beijing can slowly reverse the transfers in the same way.

4. Beijing can directly transfer wealth from the state sector to the private sector by privatizing assets and using the proceeds directly or indirectly to boost household wealth.

5. Beijing can indirectly transfer wealth from the state sector to the private sector by absorbing private-sector debt.

6. Beijing can cut investment sharply, resulting in a collapse in growth, but it can mitigate the employment impact of this collapse by hiring unemployed workers for various make-work programs and paying their salaries out of state resources.

To understand the constraints and limitations of each of these six strategies, and so to help us arrive at a prediction of how China will rebalance over the next several years, we can examine each of the six separately. Before doing so it is worth noting that rebalancing is likely to be inflationary. I discussed part of the reason for this in chapter 4, but more broadly as rebalancing forces consumption up relative to production, the ability of the economy to keep inflation down even in the face of rapid monetary growth will be reduced.

This is likely to be the case under any of the rebalancing scenarios—inflationary pressures will increase as the policies that kept inflation in check by constraining consumption growth are eased. Because rebalancing requires an elimination of the financial repression tax, it also eliminates, or at least erodes, the bifurcation of monetary policy I discussed in chapter 4.

But there is a silver lining. Until now, most Chinese inflation has been food intensive and so has resulted in significant transfers of wealth from the poor, for whom food is an important component of consumption, to the rich, for whom it isn't. Inflation under the rebalancing scenario will not necessarily affect the food sector and so is far more likely to affect the rich and middle classes. In that sense, inflation might be less socially disruptive than it has been in the past.

To return to the six rebalancing scenarios:

1. Beijing can do nothing, maintaining its high investment growth rates, until it reaches its debt capacity limits, after which a sudden stop in investment will force up the household share (albeit under conditions of negative growth).

This is the easiest set of constraints and implications to explain. In this scenario Beijing refuses to cut investment rates sharply, perhaps because it proves politically impossible, especially at the elite level. In this case, GDP growth rates will remain very high while debt levels continue to grow unsustainably.

At some point, however, Beijing reaches its debt capacity limits and is no longer able to fund continued investment. When this happens, of course, investment is no longer sufficient to generate growth (because investment drops), and GDP growth collapses.

But the story doesn't end there. It is at this point that China would fall into the self-reinforcing process of chaotic adjustment that characterized, for example, the United States in the early 1930s or Brazil in the mid-1980s. As investment falls and GDP growth grinds to a halt, rising financial distress causes businesses to fire workers. The resulting increase in unemployment causes consumption growth itself to drop, and GDP growth falls even further, resulting in more financial distress and so on in a downward spiral.

This is the worst-case scenario of rebalancing. The point worth stressing is that even though consumption growth rates drop sharply, and may even turn negative, the Chinese economy nonetheless rebalances because consumption contracts more slowly than GDP. Fired workers, after all, may lose 100 percent of their income, but they do not cut back on 100 percent of their consumption. Either they dip into their savings, or they access the savings of relatives who still have jobs, or they receive welfare transfers from the state, or they engage in other activity that may not add to GDP but nonetheless allows them to maintain some level of consumption (such as crime or emigration).

Whatever households do to maintain consumption, investment collapses much more quickly than consumption, and because GDP growth is a function of both, consumption will grow relative to GDP and the consumption share of GDP must automatically rise. China will rebalance. In the United States, for example, in 1929–1933, real gross investment fell by 91 percent, real consumption dropped by 19 percent, and real GDP dropped by 30 percent.[2] The result was catastrophic for the economy and for households, but notice that the United States did rebalance. Investment dropped sharply, and although consumption dropped, too, the consumption share of GDP rose sharply at the expense of the investment share.

But what does it mean to say that China has debt capacity limits? It may seem perfectly obvious to everyone that, at least in theory, every economic entity must have debt capacity limits. But for many analysts, surprisingly enough, the idea that China has debt capacity limits is very hard to grasp as a practical matter. This has in many ways been the most controversial part of any discussion about the limits to the Chinese growth model. No one doubts that in theory there are limits to debt creation, but because most analysts, especially those with limited historical knowledge, cannot understand how these limits occur in practice, they discount the risk of China's reaching debt capacity limits.

In chapter 7 I will discuss this further, focusing on a wholly mistaken argument made by a Goldman Sachs analyst that there is no limit to debt capacity as long as domestic savings exceed domestic investment. The assumption that even though we cannot identify the precise mechanics of debt capacity constraints we can pretty much assume they are distant is based on the historically incorrect but widely held perception that the limits of sovereign debt financing can occur only in the form of an externally driven "sudden stop." These sudden stops occur, it is believed, usually because a country is dependent on foreign financing to fund domestic investment.

For this reason, it is worth discussing a little further how the Chinese government can have a debt capacity limit. The important point to understand here is that if investment funded by debt is indeed being misallocated, and so debt is rising faster than debt-servicing capacity,

---

2   Murray Rothbard, *A History of Money and Banking in the United States: The Colonial Era to World War II* (Auburn, Ala.: Ludwig von Mises Institute, 2002), 103.

the implicit losses on the investment are not being recognized while the investment occurs, but are rather being rolled forward over the debt repayment period.

Every year, in other words, the excess of the real debt-servicing cost (once subsidies, including most importantly the financial repression subsidy, are added back) over the additional economic value created by the investment is met by an implicit transfer from some sector of the economy. This transfer, usually from the household sector, allows the investment project to cover the nominal debt-servicing cost. The most obvious way this happens is by the artificial lowering of interest rates, whereby depositors are implicitly taxed to cover borrowing costs. As the debt is serviced over time (and remember that debt is rarely repaid in China but is rolled over continuously), the losses are amortized over very long time periods.

As a result, the more investment is misallocated, the more losses are rolled forward, and the greater the total amount of losses that must be amortized in the future. This means that in order to maintain a fixed amount of economic growth, investment must rise quickly enough to generate growth as well as to pay for the earlier losses that are being amortized. Under conditions of investment misallocation, in other words, debt-funded investment must rise quickly just to maintain constant levels of growth. This, of course, is what seems to be happening in China.

At the same time, because borrowers cannot repay loans and must roll them over for many years in order to allow the losses to be amortized (that is, paid for by the household sector in the form of direct and hidden taxes), the only way to keep growth high is to engineer a rapid rise in credit funded by a rapid rise in underlying liquidity. Money must grow exponentially simply to keep the process going. That is what happened in China until very recently.

As the estimable Charlene Chu, of Fitch Ratings, put it in late 2012:

> One factor behind the recent improvement in China's economic data has been faster credit growth. Many components of bank and nonbank financing accelerated in Q312. Broad credit is on track to exceed CNY17trn in 2012, making it the fourth year in a row that net new credit will exceed a third of GDP. This accelerated pace

may last through the Q113 leadership transition, but beyond that funding and capital will place constraints on growth.[3]

As Chu warns in her piece, at some point—although it is always very hard to predict exactly when—the accumulated losses prevent deposits in the banking system from growing fast enough to cover previous losses while funding new loans. This may or may not be exacerbated by the inability of banks to fund new credit, given the inability to turn old loans into liquidity (borrowers cannot repay loans except with new loans). At this point the banking system is simply no longer capable of generating sufficiently fast credit growth to generate investment growth. When that happens, debt capacity limits have been reached.

The gradual but inexorable erosion of debt capacity is usually exacerbated by an additional, and highly pro-cyclical, process. As debt levels rise, well-informed local businessmen and the politically connected become increasingly concerned about rising instability in the banking system. Their response is disinvestment and capital flight. Of course, their response itself reduces growth further, requiring even more credit expansion to make up for it, and so further increases concerns about rising instability in the banking system. The process is self-reinforcing, which is why it is worth keeping close tabs on capital flight—both as an indication of rising instability and as an enhancer of rising instability.

There is no way of knowing at what point China is likely to reach its debt capacity limits. This limit is a function of total debt, the structure of the debt, the virulence of the various self-reinforcing mechanisms embedded in the relevant balance sheets, the incidence of exogenous and endogenous shocks, and, of course, overall confidence. We can think of debt capacity limits being reached broadly when the economic activity generated by additional loans is less than the reduction in economic activity caused by one or more of the four following conditions:

- The accumulation of earlier losses that have been rolled forward in the form of debt.

---

3   Fitch Ratings, "Chinese Banks: Credit Growth Accelerates in Q312, But Continued Aggressive Expansion Has Limits," November 8, 2012.

- Rising private-sector disinvestment caused by rising uncertainty.

- Deposit withdrawal, also caused by rising uncertainty and declining credibility (of either the banking system or, more likely, the implicit government guarantee that deposits will not be frozen or eroded).

- The strength of self-reinforcing mechanisms in which economic slowdown creates financial distress (because companies have invested on the assumption that growth will remain high and are unable to service debt if it does not). That in turn creates further economic slowdown as workers are fired and purchase orders dry up.

Because the first condition is growing at a rising rate and is sensitive to worsening economic conditions (that is, the worse the economy, the faster it grows), and the other three conditions are self-reinforcing, it is important to understand how unpredictable and sudden debt capacity limits can appear. Throughout history when a country has reached its borrowing limit, it has always happened very quickly and with little warning. The fact that it seems improbable today, in other words, has no informational content. It always seems improbable until it suddenly seems inevitable.

Given the low level of transparency in China, all of these factors are very hard to measure, but I would guess that at current rates of investment China's debt capacity is unlikely to extend much beyond three or four years. I find it unlikely, in other words, that China can maintain high levels of investment growth for longer than that without being forced into a catastrophic adjustment.

There is one additional factor to be considered in thinking about domestic debt capacity limits in China. In this context it is helpful to think about Brazil's experience during its own growth miracle (Brazil may have been the first country whose economy was described as a "miracle"), which culminated in the lost decade of the 1980s.

Brazil began to reach its own domestic debt capacity limits around the middle of the 1970s, after many years of overinvesting. There were concerns that growth would falter, but the country received a temporary reprieve from the external sector. Beginning in 1971 for a variety of reasons—many of them geopolitical—the price of oil began to rise rapidly. From $2 a barrel in 1971, oil prices surged to nearly $12 a barrel in 1975 and then to nearly $38 a barrel by 1980.

One of the consequences of this surge in oil prices was that the major oil-producing nations, most of which were unable to increase domestic investment and consumption rapidly enough to match the increase in their oil revenue, experienced dizzying increases in net domestic savings. These increased savings were exported abroad, as they must be. Much of the increase in capital exports ended up on the balance sheets of major international banks, which were hard-pressed to recycle their surge in deposits through normal lending activity.

This is when large international commercial banks turned to international lending, and especially sovereign lending, in a way that had been all but forgotten since the heady days of international lending of the 1920s. Back then the big source of recycled funds was German reparations payments and the ballooning U.S. trade surplus, just as it was the ballooning trade surpluses of OPEC nations that had to be recycled in the 1970s.

Fortunately for Brazil's president, Emílio Médici, and his 1974 successor, Ernesto Geisel—and unfortunately for Brazil—the eagerness of international banks to find new loan demand coincided with the domestic funding constraints within Brazil. As a consequence, Brazil was able to maintain its high levels of domestic investment and high growth right through the end of the 1970s, even as the United States and Europe experienced recessions and much slower growth. Brazil, like other less developed countries in Latin America and elsewhere, simply switched from domestic funding to foreign funding. This allowed Brazil to keep growth rates high through the end of the 1970s, sparking, much as we saw more recently, talk about the decoupling of the economies of the developing countries from those of the advanced economies.

Could the same thing happen to China, so that external funding relieves domestic debt capacity constraints? Of course it could. China has an excellent external credit rating and substantial reserves with which to back external claims (in fact, it can simply sell off its foreign currency assets to achieve the same effect). But for China to be a net borrower on the international markets—or a net seller of foreign assets, including U.S. government bonds, which is much the same thing—has important trade implications that might be difficult for China to absorb. As a net importer of savings China would be forced, like Brazil before it, to run a large current account deficit, probably because it would have to revalue the renminbi substantially.

Whether China would be willing to lose control of the value of the renminbi and whether it has in place an institutional framework that could make an easily manageable switch from the world's largest net exporter to among the world's largest net importers are open questions. It is not at all clear that the structure of the Chinese economy is flexible enough to permit the necessary change in the direction of capital flows.

A more important question is whether Beijing would accept the consequences. Brazil, after all, was able to use foreign borrowing to postpone the adjustment in its own investment-driven economic growth model. Most analysts agree that Brazil's investment misallocation, which had already become a problem in the late 1960s and early 1970s, increased substantially over the rest of the decade. It is not a coincidence, of course, that once external debt levels for Brazil and other less developed economies became problematic in the early 1980s, Brazil suffered a lost decade of negative growth, rising unemployment, and political instability as it was forced into rebalancing its economy and eliminating the consequences of years of misallocated investment. Foreign lending, in other words, will not solve China's investment problem. It would merely postpone the resolution while allowing the imbalances to be exacerbated and increasing the ultimate losses that have to be amortized.

2. Beijing can quickly reverse the transfers that created the imbalances by, for example, raising real interest rates sharply, forcing up the foreign exchange value of the currency by 10 to 20 percent overnight, and pushing up wages, or by lowering income and consumption taxes.

This path simply means the very rapid reversal of the process over the last decades, and especially during 2000–2010, during which the imbalances were created. Over many years, as I explained in chapters 2 and 3, the undervalued currency, repressed interest rates, and lagging wage growth (along with other hidden transfers) effectively taxed household income, with the proceeds of these "taxes" going directly to subsidize rapid growth. In the process, these "taxes" created rapid economic growth and the growing consumption imbalance.

If China were to reverse these transfers quickly, the wealth transfer that created the imbalances would immediately reverse, and this in turn would begin to eliminate the imbalances. In the Appendix to this book I describe in more specific detail exactly how a currency appreciation causes a wealth transfer from the state sector and the export sector to households. The mechanism is broadly similar for all three, and is described at the end of chapter 5.

The advantages of this strategy are very straightforward. By adjusting very quickly Beijing immediately puts a stop to the worsening of the domestic imbalances. It also immediately eliminates the strong incentives within China to waste money on a stability-threatening scale by raising the cost of capital and forcing investors to generate real returns on their investment. This, of course, also allows Beijing to finally get a grip on its ballooning debt.

But the disadvantages are also very straightforward. Eliminating the hidden subsidies abruptly would cause a massive increase in financial distress as exporters struggle with a more expensive currency, borrowers are unable to service their debt, and employers, especially the labor-intensive sector, become suddenly uncompetitive. This would almost certainly lead to a surge in unemployment as exporters and borrowers are forced to close down operations.

In the short term, under these conditions, rather than an increase in household income in the aggregate, and with it household consumption, we would probably see household income decline because the negative impact of rising unemployment would exceed the positive impact of reversing the wealth transfers. This would cause household consumption to decline, and the feedback effect of declining household consumption would almost certainly force the economy into a downward spiral, much like that of the United States during the Great Depression.

China's economy would still rebalance in this case—probably through negative growth in household income and even more negative GDP growth. That's how the U.S. economy rebalanced in the early 1930s, but China's rebalancing would be under very difficult economic and social conditions. Needless to say, this would also result in difficult political conditions.

3. Beijing can slowly reverse the transfers in the same way.

In this scenario rather than eliminate the transfers quickly, Beijing could eliminate the transfers slowly enough to give exporters, borrowers, and employers time to adjust. They need time because China's export success and economic growth depend heavily on hidden subsidies from the household sector. As Chinese businesses adapt, the adverse employment impact of removing the subsidies on export competitiveness can be counterbalanced by the positive employment impact of rising household consumption, so that there is no surge in unemployment.

The biggest advantage is that this policy fits into the gradualism that has pretty much been the default setting for most Chinese economic policymaking since the dramatic reforms put into place by Zhu Rongji, China's vice premier and premier in charge of economic policymaking until 2003. A gradual reversal of the sources of the imbalances will in principle allow China to rebalance without a surge in unemployment.

But this strategy also has a very serious negative that may make it unworkable—it accomplishes its objectives too slowly, and so it may already be too late to implement. Perhaps five or six years ago Beijing could have begun rebalancing gradually, but Beijing no longer has enough time. Remember that the total value of these subsidies is enormous—for example, I have cited studies that suggest that the value of hidden subsidies to the state-owned enterprises sector in the past decade may be anywhere from five to ten times their aggregate profitability.

This means that gradually removing the subsidies at a pace the Chinese economy can handle would result in worsening domestic imbalances for many years before there has been enough of an adjustment to reverse the imbalances. During this time the impact of those distortions—declining consumption relative to GDP, misallocated investment, and above all, rising debt—would continue to grow.

The more bad investment China accumulates, the more costly the eventual adjustment will be, and the more the adjustment process must be slowed. Gradual adjustment increases the risk of China's reaching debt capacity limits to almost near-certainty. Even though Beijing would like nothing more than to adjust gradually, that approach is too risky. An increasing number of policymakers and advisers in Beijing seem to realize this.

4. Beijing can directly transfer wealth from the state sector to the private sector by privatizing assets and using the proceeds directly or indirectly to boost household wealth. .

This is the most efficient way to increase household wealth quickly as a share of GDP, although this necessarily comes at the expense of the state sector. A contraction in the state share of GDP, however, is almost inevitable. The only question is whether it will occur in the form of an actual contraction in state assets or in the form of much slower growth in the state sector than in the overall economy. Contraction, of course, is far more efficient but also far more difficult to accomplish. Transferring wealth directly from the state sector to the household sector would almost certainly result in an actual contraction in state sector assets.

I say that a reduction in the state share of GDP is inevitable because reducing the state share of China's GDP is almost the definition of rebalancing. It is hard, in other words, to conceive of any way to increase the consumption share of GDP sustainably without increasing the household share of national income and national wealth. Perhaps not surprisingly, however, some policymakers in Beijing find it very difficult to understand why one requires the other.

The arithmetic behind the requirement is fairly straightforward. Over the past three decades, while China's GDP was growing at a furious pace, the state and corporate shares of Chinese GDP were expanding, implying an even more torrid growth in the value of state and corporate assets. It was this expansion in the state share (at the expense, of course, of the household share) that created the great imbalances in the Chinese economy, and so it is only a reversal of this process that will eliminate the imbalances.

It is worth pointing out that the real value of state assets is not nearly as great as the raw numbers imply. If investment has been misallocated and losses buried and rolled forward in the form of debt, as has almost certainly been the case, then clearly both China's GDP and, with it, the net assets of the state sector must be written down substantially.

Still, there is no question that the state possesses substantial wealth and claims on wealth. There are many ways in which wealth can be transferred to the household sector. These include the following:

- Farmers can be granted full title to their land.

- Migrants can be granted *hukou* residency, which, because it gives them legal status and rights to urban services, would act as a substantial one-off increase in their wealth.

- Beijing can strengthen the social safety net by transferring resources from the state sector, for example, by transferring ownership of state-owned enterprises to the pension funds (note, however, that if a stronger social safety net is funded by direct or indirect transfers from the household sector, as it has been to date, this scheme cannot increase the consumption share of GDP).

- Beijing can eliminate or erode monopoly pricing power through greater competition, it can impose significant charges for environmental degradation (remember that environmental degradation imposes future health and production costs on households, which must respond by increasing their savings rate), it can increase the protection of property rights, or it can make it easier, quicker, and less costly to start a business. All of these measures, and others like them, can directly or indirectly increase household perceptions of their own wealth, although many of these measures, while good in themselves, may take years to have a noticeable impact on household perceptions.

- State-owned enterprises can be sold either to foreigners or to locals, with the proceeds being distributed directly or indirectly to households.

- Vouchers granting ownership of state-owned enterprises can be distributed directly or indirectly to households.

- Privatization proceeds can be used to reduce future claims on household income. The most efficient way of doing this would be to use privatization proceeds to pay down corporate

and state debt, thus allowing the central bank to raise interest rates sharply without causing a surge in financial distress.
Higher interest rates, of course, reduce the large but hidden tax
on household savings and so boost household income at the
expense of net borrowers.

If any of these, or other, transactions result in a reduction of state
ownership and an increase in the wealth of Chinese households, especially
the wealth of poor and middle-class households, the resulting increase in
the household share of GDP will automatically increase the consumption
share of GDP. The most efficient distribution, and perhaps the easiest to
accomplish politically, involves the privatization of assets owned by the
state, the proceeds of which are used to pay down debt.

Remember that nonperforming loans (which for our purpose should
include loans that would be nonperforming if the state guarantee were
eliminated and lending rates were raised to levels that eliminated the hidden subsidy) represent a future claim on the household sector. Eliminating this future claim would cause household wealth to increase immediately—and this would most likely manifest itself as higher interest rates
paid to depositors. The combination of privatization and elimination
of subsidized capital would end the tendency for the Chinese financial
system to waste capital on a massive scale.

For all of the efficiency in transferring wealth in this way, however,
there is an enormous constraint on Beijing's ability to pull it off. The
Reverend Martin Luther King Jr. once described history rather testily as
the story of the refusal of the privileged few to give up their privileges.
Transferring assets from the state sector directly or indirectly is meaningful only in the context of a significant reform in corporate governance,
which itself involves the forgoing of important privileges. As the whole
"vested interests" debate in China suggests, and as the Minxin Pei essay
cited in chapter 5 argues, there is tremendous resistance to the loss of
power and control this would impose on many important and powerful
sectors and families within China.[4]

---

4   For an excellent historical review of what he calls "the relentless march of the central
    state," see Philip A. Kuhn, *Origins of the Modern Chinese State* (Palo Alto, Calif.: Stanford
    University Press, 2002).

It is important to note, by the way, that transferring wealth to households in the form of lower fiscal surpluses or higher fiscal deficits, as many analysts have urged, cannot be part of any meaningful rebalancing. Fiscal surpluses and deficits, after all, are simply ways of transferring wealth from one sector of the economy to another, and so both sides of the transaction matter. It is not enough that the household sector is the main "beneficiary" of such transfers. It is important also that households themselves not fund the transfers, either directly in the form of taxes or indirectly in the form of the financial repression tax (that is, the state borrows to fund the transfers).

There must be an actual transfer of wealth from the state to the households. This means that if the state runs a fiscal deficit, in order for this to represent a real increase in the household share of GDP, the deficit must be financed by the sale of state assets, not by borrowing. This is one of the key mistakes that too many economists make when they discuss forms of transfers to the households.

5. Beijing can indirectly transfer wealth from the state sector to the private sector by absorbing private-sector debt.

This is what Japan effectively did as a fundamental part of its rebalancing after 1990, when government debt rose from roughly 20 percent of GDP to the current 200–250 percent of GDP. The government effectively absorbed the bad loans in the banking sector. Government debt expanded rapidly, while private-sector debt contracted. This was the equivalent of a transfer of debt from the private to the public balance sheet.

This may at first seem counterintuitive as a form of wealth transfer, but remember that my taking over your debt has the same net impact on your wealth and mine as my giving you my assets. In either case I am transferring wealth to you. How does Beijing's absorption of private debt benefit the household sector? Mainly because as corporate debt is absorbed by the state, it allows corporations to stay in business (and not fire workers) and expand even while wages and borrowing costs are rising (and it is the rising wages and deposit rates that will increase household income).

The great advantage of this form of rebalancing is that it is very easy to do politically because it does not entail taking away assets, or the control over those assets, from any of the powerful families or groups that control the country. But this strategy comes with an important cost. As we saw in the case of Japan, after a decade or so, this strategy leaves the government struggling with too much debt. The debt burden itself becomes the biggest impediment to growth, because the direct or hidden taxes required to service it reduce consumption-driven growth, and the size of the debt limits policy choices for the government.

This strategy also prevents the right kind of interest rate adjustment, because the burgeoning government debt forces the central bank to keep interest rates low or risk government insolvency. In the end interest rates must adjust one way or the other to end the financial repression tax (if they do not, consumption cannot rise in relative terms). The only way Japan was able to raise real interest rates to their "natural" level, and so prevent the worsening of investment misallocation, was through annual GDP growth rates of less than 1 percent caused by a sharp drop in investment.[5]

Because the gap between the nominal risk-free lending rate and the nominal growth rate is essentially the measure of the subsidy that net depositors provide to net borrowers, as growth rates dropped, so did Japan's financial repression tax. If Beijing cannot allow interest rates to rise to meet high GDP growth rates, rebalancing is likely to occur only in the form of much lower GDP growth rates and burgeoning debt, as happened in Japan.

6. Beijing can cut investment sharply, resulting in a collapse in growth, but it can mitigate the employment impact of this collapse by hiring unemployed workers for various make-work programs and paying their salaries out of state resources.

While hiring unemployed and unproductive workers eliminates or reduces the social and political cost of restructuring, it can also mean a transfer of wealth from the state to the workers. If this transfer is paid for by the household sector (through explicit taxes or through hidden

---

5 Akio Mikuni and R. Taggart Murphy, *Japan's Policy Trap: Dollars, Deflation, and the Crises of Japanese Finance* (Washington, D.C.: Brookings Institution Press, 2002).

taxes, like higher financial repression taxes caused by expanded government borrowing), it will have a minimal impact on household consumption. If it is paid for out of state assets, it will improve household consumption.

The key, again, is how the payments are funded. To summarize:

- If wage costs for unproductive workers are paid for in the form of a fiscal deficit, debt will continue to rise too quickly and Beijing runs the risk of lumbering into our first scenario, in which its debt capacity limits are reached.
- If wage costs for unproductive workers are paid for in the form of direct or hidden taxes on the household sector, it will leave aggregate household consumption unchanged as a share of GDP because higher income for the underemployed workers will be matched by lower disposable income for employed workers.
- If wage costs for unproductive workers are paid for by the liquidation of state assets, there will be a real increase in the household income and consumption shares of GDP.

In the end we always get back to the need to transfer wealth from the state to the household sector. The advantage of rebalancing in this way, by simply moving unproductive workers onto government payrolls, is that it is gradual and protects workers from rising unemployment. The disadvantage is that it is economically inefficient. Hiring and paying unproductive workers can be only a temporary solution to the rebalancing problem. More importantly, it doesn't address the fundamental problem of how these payments are to be funded.

HOW WILL BEIJING CHOOSE?

As I see it, these six are ultimately the only scenarios—or at least the major set of scenarios—Beijing can follow over the next few years. If it does nothing—which is to say, it follows the first scenario—China will rebalance anyway, but in the form of a debt crisis. If it wants to avoid a debt crisis, it will have to choose one or more from among the next five scenarios.

For example, we can posit the following. Beijing can choose an intermediate path between the second and third scenarios and raise interest rates sharply over the next two or three years while also raising the value of the renminbi by some large amount, say 10–15 percent, in an overnight maxi-revaluation.

To protect workers from the resulting surge in unemployment, Beijing can instruct state-owned companies and local governments temporarily to hire a huge number of workers for make-work programs (the sixth scenario) and initially pay for this by increasing government borrowing (the fifth scenario). At the same time it can begin a program of privatization (the fourth scenario), which should include transferring ownership of land to peasants, and selling off assets, and using the proceeds to shore up the social safety net and to pay down debt in the banking system.

This would certainly work economically to rebalance China in a way that guarantees fairly high growth rates over the rest of the decade, but is it politically possible? Here I would defer to political analysts, who might argue that the scale of privatization required is not possible politically. In that case China would end up being forced into rebalancing mainly via the fifth scenario, with a long-term surge in government debt.

And this is the point. If we accept that our original assumptions are correct—that China is misallocating investment and must rebalance toward a greater reliance on consumption, and that the low household consumption share of GDP reflects the low household income share of GDP—then we must agree that China has no choice but to follow one or more of the paths described above. If privatization is not an option, then a collapse in the economy caused by a rapid adjustment in interest rates and the currency (the second scenario) might be. If that is ruled out, then perhaps the outcome will be a surge in government debt (the fifth scenario again), and so on.

These are the economic constraints that limit the choices Beijing can make. It doesn't matter what anyone thinks Beijing will do or what anyone wants Beijing to do; if the plan violates the economic constraints, it simply cannot be done.

CHAPTER 7

HOW TO BE A CHINA BULL

In the many debates I have had on the subject of China's adjustment, and in conversations with other senior officials, my counterparts have largely constrained themselves to three arguments to support claims of continued very high growth in China. First, they presented historical data showing rapid Chinese growth rates in the past three decades and proposed that this was evidence of rapid Chinese growth rates in the next two decades.

Second, they asserted that because past predictions of failure have all turned out to be wrong (a widespread misperception, by the way, to which I will return), future predictions must also be wrong. And third, they produced a number of what seem to me largely circular arguments—such as the claim that urbanization leads to growth and growth to urbanization, and so the process must continue. Or the claim that because productivity has soared, past investments in the aggregate have been justified, even though the data "proving" the increase in productivity implicitly assume that past investments have been economically justified.

For a typical example of this kind of argument, Hong Kong's *South China Morning Post* carried the following article in late 2012 by a seemingly plugged-in analyst, confident of brighter days ahead:

> I can't predict when the economy will rebound, but perhaps it is time for analysts to look at the longer term. Where will China stand in 20 years?

First, let's examine the prediction that its gross domestic product will become the largest in the world within a decade, and its economy will continue to improve over the next two decades. *The Economist* expects Chinese GDP to surpass America's by 2018, and even if China's growth rate were to drop to 5 per cent, this transition would only be delayed until 2021. Therefore, there is little need to worry about current GDP growth falling to 8 per cent. Other forecasts of when the transition will happen include 2016 (the International Monetary Fund) and 2020 (the Chinese Academy of Social Sciences).

… Second, the renminbi is forecast to become freely convertible within 10 years and possibly will be competing with the US dollar in two decades. In recent discussions, it was thought this first step could be realised in five years. I believe it will probably happen by 2020, or when Chinese GDP becomes the largest in the world.

… Third, it is said that Hong Kong is likely to exceed New York as a global financial centre within 20 years. As China's economy continues to grow and develop, the realisation of the first two predictions will provide a great boost for Hong Kong, and it is expected to gradually become the dominant global financial centre.

… Fourth, some predict that Chinese enterprises will make up more than half of the Fortune Global 500 companies in two decades, and China will be a global manufacturing power. This year, there are 73 Chinese companies (79 if Taiwanese companies are included) on the list, a significant increase from only 11 a decade ago.

… Fifth, China is expected to make significant progress in the field of science, technology and education, and the University of Hong Kong is likely to be ranked among the top 10 in the world within two decades. According to a study by the science and technology think tank Battelle, China currently accounts for about 15 per cent of the total share of global research and development spending, and it will surpass the US spending within a decade.

… Thus, there is every reason to be optimistic about China's economic prospects over the next two decades.[1]

---

1 G. Bin Zhao, "Brighter Days Ahead for China's Economy," *South China Morning Post*, September 17, 2012.

This is very typical of the kinds of bullish arguments for China made even recently. Notice, however, that the reasons for predicting that the Chinese economy will be much stronger than many people currently expect consist largely of citing a series of earlier predictions. This doesn't seem like a very robust argument, and although I have only excerpted the article, I think anyone who reads the full article would agree that I did not leave out anything more substantial.

I don't mean to pick on the author, a prominent former consultant and currently editor of *China's Economy & Policy*, especially since it is an op-ed piece, in which it is always hard to make substantial arguments. But I hear this kind of reasoning a lot. The "proof" that China will grow very rapidly in the next decade, the reasoning goes, is that many experts have predicted that China will grow very rapidly in the next decade.

Unfortunately, predictions of this sort are notoriously unreliable, and economists seem to be especially bad at predicting turning points. Karl Marx once noted that when the train of history hits a curve, intellectuals tend to fall off the train. Intellectual inertia keeps them moving in the same direction, even though the train is no longer going there. Earlier predictions, Marx suggests, are pretty useless in a debate about whether we are at a turning point.

But it is not just inertia. Many China bulls have gleefully insisted that "experts" have been warning of economic problems in China for two decades and have always been wrong. Therefore, they argue, any further warning is also likely to be wrong. Aside from the fact that this claim is completely irrelevant—after all, premature warnings are not wrong, they are simply premature—it is also based on a very superficial understanding of the economic track record.

In fact, China has been through many crises, just as experts predicted. But these crises never showed up in the form of sustained periods of much slower economic activity. This was not because policymakers had unprecedented skills in resolving economic problems, or because the crisis wasn't severe, but rather because policymakers had access to a very powerful, albeit dangerous, tool that allowed them to overcome growth slowdowns. The crises occurred as predicted, but they were overcome by policies that merely postponed the ultimate cost.

This, by the way, is not just a China problem. Analysts who had been warning about increasing instability in the U.S. financial markets, beginning with the Internet bubble in the 1990s, were made to look foolish at first because the great reckoning never seemed to arrive. But they weren't wrong in their predictions. What happened instead was that policymakers, especially the Federal Reserve Bank, took steps to prevent the full unwinding of these financial excesses. Monetary policies engineered to protect the economy did not protect the economy so much as create new sources of financial instability. But as the U.S. financial crisis beginning in 2007–2008 showed, while the economic impact of each source of financial instability was muted, it was not eliminated, and eventually the U.S. economy ended up paying in full for the financial excesses of the previous twenty years.

The same thing has happened in China. Many of the predicted crises did occur, but their resolution was postponed and the adverse impact on the Chinese economy was hidden, not eliminated. It is important to realize that China's spectacular growth in the past thirty years, and its ability to forge its way forcefully through periods of difficult economic adjustment, was made possible mainly by the ability of policymakers to control credit and unleash waves of investment whenever it was needed. This allowed Beijing to keep growth rates high no matter what the circumstance and no matter how well or poorly the leadership had managed earlier domestic problems.

HOW TO BE BULLISH ON GROWTH

China, for example, avoided a surge in unemployment when it restructured the hugely inefficient state-owned industries in the 1990s by sharply increasing infrastructure investment. It used more investment to smooth over the social dislocations caused by a rigid and antiquated political structure. It eased political conflicts and factional fighting by directing billions of dollars of investment into pet projects. Much of the money was subsequently siphoned off by the politically connected. This strategy even protected the country from crises. China grew vigorously through the Asian crisis of 1997, the Chinese banking crisis a few years later, and, more recently, the collapse of the global economy in 2007–

2008, and the collapse in China's trade account in 2009–2010. In each case unrestricted access to the savings of the country allowed Beijing to power growth by pouring those savings into any project it chose.

But not much longer. Investment is nearing its limit, and in fact excess investment has itself become China's greatest economic problem. Many years of high and often wasted investment—the nearly inevitable consequence of unrestricted access to a country's savings—has resulted in debt growing much faster than debt-servicing capacity. More investment only worsens the country's debt problem. That is why past success in keeping growth high tells us nothing about Beijing's future ability to keep growth high.

I am not saying, of course, that there is no credible argument to be bullish on China. There may well be one, but in order to argue that there will not be a sharp slowdown in Chinese growth, I would propose that it is not enough to claim that some expert or the other has predicted that Chinese growth will not slow down. Nor can the argument be made (which is much the same thing, I suspect) that China has grown rapidly in the past, so it must grow rapidly in the future. And finally, and most foolishly, it cannot be asserted, as I have heard many times, that Beijing leaders cannot tolerate growth below 7.5 percent, therefore growth will not drop below 7.5 percent.

To counter the current level of pessimism with the bullish case, it seems to me that three specific questions must be answered. The first question, of course, has to do with debt. How much debt is there in China, in other words, whose debt-servicing costs (adjusted upward to eliminate interest rate and other subsidies) exceed the economic value creation of the projects funded by that debt?

Just as importantly, analysts need to show which sector of the economy will be forced to pay for the difference. Remember that excess debt doesn't pay for itself, and if you cannot identify who is paying, then you haven't completed the analysis of the problem. Many people, for example, argue that bad debt today isn't a problem for the same reason that China "grew out" of its debt crisis of the late 1990s. This is nonsense. China did not grow out of the debt. It merely forced the cost of the crisis onto the household sector through repressed interest rates and a wide spread between the deposit and lending rates.

More generally throughout modern history, and in nearly every economic system, whether we are talking about China, the United States, France, Brazil, or any other country, there has really been only one meaningful way to resolve banking crises. Whenever nonperforming loans or contingent liabilities surge to the point where the solvency of the banking system is threatened, the regulators ensure that wealth is transferred in sufficient amounts from the household sector to borrowers or banks to replenish bank capital and bring them back to solvency. The household sector, in other words, always pays to clean up the banks.

There are many ways to make them pay. In some cases, for example in the United States before the 1930s, banks simply defaulted and their depositors absorbed the full loss. In this case it was the actual bank depositors, mainly households, who directly bore the full cost of the losses, in the form of reduced repayment of their deposits—or sometimes no repayment.

Largely because this kind of system creates incentives for bank runs, regulators developed alternative systems, by which governments guaranteed deposits and otherwise bailed out the banks, paying for the bailout by raising taxes. The household sector still paid for the losses, but it did so largely in the form of taxes, and the losses were spread throughout the population rather than concentrated among the bank depositors.

Of course, this way of bailing out the banks is politically unpopular and always leads to uncomfortable calls to punish the banks for their behavior. If the regulators are given more time to clean up the banks, they can use other, less obvious and so less politically unpopular, ways to do the same thing, such as by managing interest rates. In the United States and Europe, it is fairly standard for the central bank to engineer a steep yield curve by forcing down short-term rates. Since banks borrow short from their depositors and lend long to their customers, the banks are effectively guaranteed a spread, at the expense, of course, of depositors. Over many years, the depositors end up recapitalizing the banks, usually without realizing it.[2]

---

2   Although we don't completely agree on how the banking crisis of the 1990s was actually resolved, Carl Walter and Fraser Howie, *Red Capitalism: The Fragile Financial Foundation of China's Extraordinary Rise* (Singapore: Wiley & Sons, 2011), is indispensable in

There are two additional ways to recapitalize banks that are used by countries, like China, whose financial systems are highly controlled. One is to mandate a wide spread between the lending and deposit rates. In China that spread has been an extremely high 3.0–3.5 percentage points, and this spread represents, effectively, guaranteed profits for the banks. The other, and more effective, way is to force down the lending and deposit rates sharply in order to minimize the loan burden and spur investment. This is also what China has done in the past decade. These low interest rates help resolve nonperforming loans by granting continual debt forgiveness to borrowers.

How so? Because if interest rates are set at a level lower than the natural rate, every year the borrower is effectively granted debt forgiveness equal to the difference between the two. By most standards, even ignoring the borrower's credit risk, the lending rate in China during the past decade is likely to have been anywhere from 4 to 6 percentage points too low. Over five to ten years or more, this is an awful lot of debt forgiveness.

These all sound like radically different ways of addressing insolvent banking systems, but make no mistake, they are all simply different ways of spreading the cost of bank insolvency among households. It is important to remember this in the face of the widely held but incorrect belief that China was able to grow out of its last banking crisis, when the share of nonperforming loans in the Chinese banking system was estimated to range from 20 to 40 percent of total loans, at a relatively low cost to the economy.

Many analysts believe that it was a combination of explicit steps to recapitalize the banks—directly by injecting capital and indirectly by purchasing bad loans at very high prices—and very rapid GDP growth, matched by even more rapid loan growth, that resolved China's banking crisis. But, in fact, it was not growth and good management that resolved the crisis. It was hidden transfers from the household sector to recapitalize the banks and grant debt forgiveness to the borrowers.

This "solved" the banking crisis, but at the expense of the household sector and so directly caused China's household consumption rate to

---

understanding China's financial sector reforms and the vulnerabilities that remained after the reforms.

collapse from 46 percent of GDP in 2000, already a very low number, to 35 percent of GDP in 2010. But bad debt this time around cannot be resolved in the same way if consumption is expected to power economic growth, rather than lag behind it as it did during the period in which the banking crisis was resolved. Household consumption is already too low and debt levels too high to permit a repeat.

INVESTMENT AND CONSUMPTION

And remember that in measuring China's debt, official government debt levels are not what matter. We must include contingent liabilities, we must account for hidden and informal banking debt, and we must consider the further balance sheet consequences of an economic slowdown. The latter is especially important. For example, what is the total level of commodity stockpiles in China, in raw and in finished form, and implicitly stockpiled in unsold inventory? Unsold apartments, for example, include a great deal of copper. How much of this is backed by debt, and if prices decline sharply (as economic growth itself declines), what will the net debt impact be?

If we are to proffer a much more bullish story on Chinese growth, we must explicitly recognize and reconcile contingent bad debts. They must be resolved, and one sector of the economy or the other will necessarily be on the hook to make up the difference between the real cost of the debt and the economic value created by the debt.[3]

The first question, on debt, is of course closely related to the second important question, which has to with investment. Are there significant areas in which Beijing can and will invest so that the real increase in economic value creation exceeds the unsubsidized cost of capital?

This question is a little more complicated than simply looking for good investment opportunities in China and then assuming that the bulk of future investments will go there. In many areas, such as primary educa-

---

3   The most important work on the relationship between debt and the functioning of the economy is that of Hyman Minsky. See, for example, his *Can "It" Happen Again? Essays on Instability and Finance* (Armonk, N.Y.: M. E. Sharpe, 1982).

tion and social housing, the value of investment is likely to be positive in the very long term. But it is important to remember that these don't pay off their investments for at least a generation or so, in which case they do not help address the current imbalances.

On the contrary, they make the imbalances worse for many years before they start reducing debt and rebalancing the household sector. The only kind of investment growth that can help China address its debt overhang is investment in projects in which the increase in productivity in the next five to ten years exceeds the unsubsidized cost of the investment. If it doesn't, the transfers from either the household sector or the state sector needed to amortize losses must continue and even grow.

This is a very simple but powerful condition. Any debt-funded investment that does not satisfy this condition will make the debt problem worse. The bullish case must identify trillions of dollars of such potential investment. But even if the investments are identified, this is not enough. We must show that in spite of constraints that led to uneconomic investment in the past, these "good" investments are likely to be made on a substantial scale. The incentive structures and institutional constraints that prefer large-scale investments in real estate, railroads, expansion of manufacturing capacity, and so on must now allow a switch to a very different form of investment altogether, with all this implies about changes in governance.

The third question is about future sources of growth. Because it is now widely accepted that investment growth must slow sharply (unless we can find—and execute in spite of political constraints—many trillions of dollars of these new "good" investments), it is obvious that only a surge in consumption growth can replace investment. So the question for the bulls is: how specifically will China cause consumption to surge? Beijing has tried to force up the growth rate of consumption since at least 2005, and it has not been able to do so. More worrisome, there is some evidence that the growth rate of consumption may be dropping.

But—and this is just arithmetic unless we assume explosive growth in the external sector—if investment growth drops, consumption growth must rise by a much larger number (because consumption is much lower than investment) to maintain the same level of overall growth. If you cannot specify the mechanism that will cause consumption to grow much faster relative to GDP—and logically this can happen only if income grows much faster or if consumer debt surges—unless you deny that China must reduce investment growth, you have no choice but to accept that GDP growth will slow sharply.

Any China bull who does not address these three questions is missing the point. I am not suggesting that there is no answer to these questions. Chapter 6 discussed economically efficient, albeit politically difficult, steps China can take to address both debt and consumption growth. Any bullish forecast, however, that cannot come up with very specific assurances that one or all of these three questions will be answered is as useful as forecasts in 1989 and 1990 that Japan would get over its domestic imbalances and continue growing by 7 percent annually for the next two decades simply because it had done so in the past.

RECLASSIFYING INVESTMENT

As an aside, one of the predictions cited in the *South China Morning Post* article above to "prove" future rapid Chinese growth is that the "*Economist* expects Chinese GDP to surpass America's by 2018." The *Economist* has tended to be very much in the bullish camp on Chinese economic prospects. In late 2012, for example, the magazine published an article on China wondering if Chinese growth policies are more Keynesian or more Hayekian (I think they are neither):

> Moreover, investment that adds little to a society's stock of productive assets is not necessarily malinvestment. Michael Buchanan and Yin Zhang of Goldman Sachs say that some Chinese investment is best seen as "quasi-consumption." In this category they place things like earthquake-proof schools and more comfortable metro lines. Instead of adding to the economy's productive capacity, these assets provide a flow of services (such as reassurance to parents and relaxed travel) directly to consumers. In this respect they are more akin to consumer durables, like washing machines or cars, than to iron-ore mines or steel plants.
>
> As a rough gauge of the size of quasi-consumption, the Goldman economists add up China's investment in house building and "social infrastructure," such as utilities, transport, water conservation,

education and health care. Reclassifying this spending as consumption would increase China's household consumption to 53 per cent of GDP last year, compared with only 35 per cent in the official statistics…

Hayek thought that badly conceived investment would only result in a worse bust later. This belief is shared by many bearish commentators on China's economy. But China's high investment is backed by even higher saving. As a consequence, China does not need its investment to generate high returns in order to pay back external creditors. China has, in effect, already set aside the resources that will be lost if its investments turn sour.[4]

To take the first two paragraphs, the debate about what should or should not be qualified as consumption gets a little wobbly at times and almost always misses the point. There are at least three problems with the argument as it is presented above.

First, it is a little hard to see the point of reclassifying investment outlays as consumption simply because they ultimately serve households, unless it is merely to try to make consumption numbers look better than they are. Ultimately the point of all investment is to increase household consumption, and yet there is nonetheless a distinction between consumption and investment that is useful and valid in understanding the mechanics of growth.

Adjusting China's numbers may make consumption seem higher, but in that case we should adjust every country's numbers in the same way and the result would be the same: China would still have the most unbalanced economy in the world, and it would still urgently need to raise household consumption. The proof? Because the current account surplus is by definition the excess of savings over investment, any country with a high investment level should have a current account deficit—unless its savings rate is also very high.

For a country with the highest investment ever recorded to have a huge current account surplus implies that it must have an extraordinarily high savings rate, which is the same as saying that it has an extraordinari-

---

4 Free Exchange, "Hayek on the Standing Committee," *Economist*, September 15, 2012.

ly low consumption rate. Reclassifying some investment as consumption reduces somewhat the extent of the savings imbalances, but the numbers are still so high that reclassifying them cannot change the underlying problem.

Second, the impact on growth, which is the whole point of the exercise, will be unchanged by how we classify the spending. As China reduces investment, consumption must grow to replace it. Are we suggesting that it will be easier for China to increase the investment that it wants to reclassify as consumption? Fine, maybe it will be, but how will this increased investment be paid for? This is the key point, and it doesn't matter whether we classify the spending as investment, consumption, or indeed anything else.

If this increased spending is paid by direct and hidden taxes on the household sector, as most spending and investment in China currently are, it simply makes it all the more difficult for household consumption to increase. Transfers from households to fund government spending are at the heart of the Chinese growth imbalances, and reclassifying those transfers does nothing to help the problem. Only reversing them will solve the problem. If the increased spending is paid for by liquidating assets in the state sector, then it also really doesn't matter how this spending is classified. As long as it results in a transfer of wealth from the state sector to the household sector, China will rebalance.

And third, there can be a huge difference between the value of inputs—which is how all this is measured—and the actual economic value of what is created, and this gets us right back to the problem of overinvestment. If a local government spends $2 billion on the subway system, but creates only $1 billion of value (increased economic activity over the life of the subway), reported "reclassified" consumption might rise by the former number, but real "reclassified" consumption goes up only by the latter number. In that case the value of the new consumption number is overstated in the same way that the value of investment has been overstated.

The article does point out that not all past investment in infrastructure is wasted, but of course this is a trivial point and one that no one doubts. The relevant point is very different. As long as debt in the aggregate rises faster than debt-servicing capacity in the aggregate, it cannot be sustained. One way or the other, the difference must be covered by transfers from either the household sector, in which case the imbalances are getting worse, or by the state sector, in which case rebalancing is occurring but the original political problem—which in China is referred to as the problem of "vested interests"—still exists.

THROWING AWAY YOUR SAVINGS

The biggest problem with the *Economist* article, however, is actually not with the first two paragraphs in the section that I cite but rather in the last. To repeat:

> But China's high investment is backed by even higher saving. As a consequence, China does not need its investment to generate high returns in order to pay back external creditors. China has, in effect, already set aside the resources that will be lost if its investments turn sour.

This claim illustrates, I think, some of the widespread confusion about what "savings" means. Because the misunderstanding is so widespread, and even seems intuitively appealing, it is worth examining further. The passage seems to assume that the main economic problem facing a developing country is paying back external creditors.

But this isn't the case. External debt is generally is a problem for smaller countries, but as the Carmen Reinhart and Kenneth Rogoff book, *This Time Is Different*, makes clear (and this is something that most financial historians already knew), most economic or financial crises are domestic, not external.[5] It is true that many of the crises in the 1980s and 1990s were external debt crises, and this has colored our view of what a financial crisis is, but this shouldn't lead us to think that countries have crises only if their savings are insufficient to cover investment (that is, they are running a current account deficit).

After all, the United States had no problem paying back its very limited external debt in the 1930s and Japan had no problem paying its very limited external debt in the 1990s. In both cases, domestic savings

---

5 Carmen Reinhart and Kenneth Rogoff, *This Time Is Different: Eight Centuries of Financial Folly* (Princeton, N.J.: Princeton University Press, 2011).

far exceeded domestic investment—or, to put it in the same terms as the *Economist*, their high investment was backed up by even higher savings. And yet both suffered tremendous slowdowns in economic growth, and the United States had a financial crisis.

Likewise, China, of course, will also have no problem paying back its current levels of external debt, but losses do not occur when a country borrows in foreign currency to fund investments. They occur when the country invests in projects that are not economically viable, no matter how they are funded.

What is more important, it is not meaningful to say that China's high investment is "backed" by higher savings, and this is perhaps one of the most dangerous and confused assumptions about financial risk in China. In order to fund investment, the Chinese growth model forces up savings by constraining consumption growth (a higher savings rate is the same thing as a lower consumption rate), just as the economist Alexander Gerschenkron prescribed in the 1950s and 1960s. But once investment is misallocated (or "malinvested," as the *Economist* prefers), higher savings is not a solution to the problem but a manifestation of the problem.

Perhaps the easiest way to prove this is with a simple thought experiment. Let us assume that Beijing decides immediately to tax half of Chinese household income and to use the money to build a bunch of useless bridges to nowhere. Would this be good for China? Certainly not, and the impact would be more debt and slower future growth as the cost of the excess debt was absorbed. What happens to the investment rate? It goes up, of course, along with GDP.

But what happens to the savings rate? It also goes up. Why? Because if we cut the disposable income of Chinese households in half, presumably we would also cut consumption by nearly that amount. Because savings is simply GDP minus consumption, savings will soar. Notice that none of the funding for these bridges came from abroad.

And notice that the condition—that savings exceed investment—will still be met, and by definition as long as China runs a current account surplus, savings must exceed investment. And yet it doesn't help. Wasting money is always value destroying, and the fact that it is funded by domestic savings (as Japan did in the 1980s, the USSR in the 1950s and 1960s, the United States in the 1920s, and Brazil before 1975) or foreign savings (as in Latin America after 1975 and much of Asia in the 1990s) makes little difference except in the resolution. Externally funded misallocated investment is subject to "sudden stops." Domestically funded misallocated investment may or may not be, depending on the structure of the domestic financial system. But whether projects are funded domestically or externally, there are debt capacity constraints.

THE BULL ARGUMENT CANNOT IGNORE HIDDEN BAD DEBT

So to say that China has already set aside the resources to pay for the losses because its savings rate exceeds its investment rate is, I think, meaningless, especially if it implies that somehow the impact of this wasted investment is in the past and not the future. China has no more set aside the cost of the losses than Brazil had done so at the end of the 1970s, prior to its own lost decade. The losses are simply buried in the debt.

An unrecognized past loss, no matter how it is funded, must be recognized at some point in the future. On this point I think neither Hayek nor Keynes would disagree. In the end, the strongest indication about whether the current Chinese growth model is no longer providing sustainable growth is whether debt is rising faster than debt-servicing capacity. This is where the debate must focus. Or to cite John Mills in his 1867 paper, "On Credit Cycles and the Origin of Commercial Panics": "Panics do not destroy capital; they merely reveal the extent to which it has been previously destroyed by its betrayal into hopelessly unproductive works."

If capital has been destroyed in the past, and that destruction is currently unrecognized, it must be recognized in the future, like it or not. This recognition can occur in the form of what Mills called a panic (what we would call a financial crisis), but given the stickiness of deposits in the Chinese banking system I don't think this is likely to be the case in China. It can also occur in the form of many years of much slower growth in GDP, as those losses are ground away through excess debt repayment.

But one way or the other, the recognition of those losses will occur. If anyone wants to continue to be very bullish about Chinese growth prospects over the next decade, there certainly is an argument to be made. But it seems to me that China bulls must explicitly address and answer the following questions:

- How much debt is there whose real cost exceeds the economic value created by the debt, which sector of the economy will pay for the excess, and what mechanism will ensure the necessary wealth transfer?

- What projects can be identified that will allow hundreds of billions of dollars, or even trillions of dollars, of investment whose wealth creation in the short and medium term will exceed the real cost of the debt, and what is the mechanism for ensuring that these investments will get made?

- What specific mechanisms can be implemented to increase the growth rate of household consumption, and how do they increase the growth rate?

THE ARITHMETIC OF REBALANCING

Before concluding this book, I propose to do something a smart economist should never do, and that is to make a verifiable prediction in writing. How fast will China grow in the decade following the ascension of the new leadership in 2013? I think it is possible, based on plausible assumptions, to estimate China's growth rate for the adjustment period, or at least to estimate the upper limit of growth assuming the transition is well managed.

There is one caveat I should point out with any long-term projection of Chinese economic growth during the adjustment. We have a varied history of countries that have experienced growth miracles—remember my having cited in chapter 1 Robert Aliber's half-jesting reworking of Andy Warhol: "In the future every country will grow rapidly for fifteen years." In every case of rapid unbalanced growth, even long before the countries were forced into their economic crises and adjustments, there were skeptics who did not believe the growth was sustainable and predicted a difficult adjustment.

In every case that I have been able to identify, however, even the most pessimistic predictions seriously underestimated the actual slowdown in growth, although in some cases (for example, Japan) the social consequences of the slowdown were not nearly as bad as many would have predicted. It wasn't until well after World War II, for example, that economists realized that despite Germany's impressive-seeming economic performance during the 1930s, the country was on the verge of bank-ruptcy by 1939. In the early 1960s, to take another example, even the most skeptical of economists did not expect the economic collapse of the USSR in the 1980s.

The Brazilian and, more generally, Latin American miracles of the 1960s and 1970s bred many skeptics, but as far as I know no one pre-dicted the severity of the lost decade of the 1980s. In spite of the sheer magnitude of Japan's imbalances, even deeply skeptical economists like Paul Krugman talked about five years of growth below 3 percent as the cost of the Japanese adjustment (and as late as 1994 the IMF had "down-graded" Japan's long-term growth rate to 4 percent), when in fact Japan suffered two decades of growth below 1 percent annually.

The point is that economists have had historically a great deal of trouble in correctly adjusting their expectations during major transitions. We are always astonished both by the extent of growth during the growth period and by the extent of the slowdown during the adjustment period. I have even argued in an earlier book that our surprise in both direc-tions may be at least partly explained by the structure of national balance sheets as the growth period is funded.[6] This does not mean, of course, that China will necessarily confound even the skeptics, but it is worth recognizing the extent to which history suggests that even the skeptics tend to get it wrong.

So what is my growth projection for China? In early 2012 the *Econo-mist* argued that China would become the world's largest economy by 2018. I offered the editors a bet. They accepted my bet and added an-other. I had argued several times that China's average annual growth rates for the decade after 2102–2013 would not exceed 3–4 percent, and they challenged me on this:

> Michael Pettis has challenged us to a bet. For those of you who don't know him, Mr Pettis is a finance professor at Peking Univer-sity's Guanghua School of Management and a frequent blogger. He would like to bet that China's dollar GDP (calculated at market

---

6 Michael Pettis, *The Volatility Machine: Emerging Economies and the Threat of Financial Collapse* (New York: Oxford University Press, 2001).

exchange rates) will NOT surpass America's in 2018. That is the year that China's economy will overtake America's if you stick with the default assumptions in our most recent interactive chart, which allows you to plug in your own guesstimates of future growth and inflation in the two countries, as well as the exchange rate between them.

When he is not fretting about China's economy, Mr Pettis runs his own record label in Beijing (Maybe Mars). If we lose the bet, he'd like us to invite one of his indie-rock bands to perform at an *Economist* conference. If we win, he has to give us a record deal (not really).

Free Exchange is happy to accept the bet, one blog with another. We would also love to see a band like Ourself Beside Me, Bird-striking or The Offset: Spectacles playing at an *Economist* confer-ence.... We'd also like to propose a counter bet. Mr Pettis reckons China's "average growth in this decade will barely break 3%." He is definitely smarter than your average bear, but that prediction looks aggressively pessimistic to us. We'd like to bet that growth will break 3%. (Let's say we win if it exceeds 3.5% on average in constant yuan over the decade.)[7]

My 3–4 percent projection as the upper limit of average growth over the next decade may seem surprising. Consensus growth estimates have certainly dropped sharply in recent years from the near-delirious predic-tions of 9–10 percent, but many economists are still predicting growth rates over the next decade of more than twice my projected level. While the consensus for annual long-term growth may have dropped by late 2012 to 5–7 percent, many of the traditionally more bullish economists are still projecting growth rates between 7 and 9 percent.

Ma Jun of Deutsche Bank, for example, claims that China's potential growth rate is 8–8.5 percent.[8] Dong Tao of Credit Suisse wrote "we

---

7 "You're On," Free Exchange, *Economist*, March 30, 2012. I apologize for including the entire entry, but I never turn down an opportunity to advertise the astonishingly good new music scene in Beijing.

8 "China: What Kind of U-Shaped Recovery?" Deutsche Bank, October 2012.

believe China will be growing around 7–8% in the coming years."[9] Arthur Kroeber of Gavekal Dragonomics Research in a February 2011 presentation for clients predicted that during 2010 to 2020 China would grow at around 8 percent. Chiwoong Lee at Goldman Sachs predicted that China's long-term growth rate will "drop" to 7.5–8.5 percent.[10] Stephen Green of Standard Chartered argued that just for poorer provinces to catch up to the income levels of the richer provinces should guarantee growth rates over the next five years of at least 7 percent.[11]

More worrisome than this sell-side optimism, perhaps, is that in an October 2012 white paper the Australian government projected that from 2012 to 2025 China would grow on average by 7 percent.[12] This is especially disturbing because after so many years of benefiting disproportionately from China's very lopsided investment-driven growth—and accepting the consequent domestic distortions that have relatively weakened the manufacturing sector at the expense of the extractive sectors—the Australian government seems to be eager to double its bet just as it becomes clear that China must face a difficult adjustment and as policymakers in Beijing debate how to abandon the old growth model and how quickly to do it.

Mind you, they are not alone. In January 2013 U.S. investment bank Jefferies predicted boldly (its word), and with admirable precision, that China's economy would grow by 6.9 percent a year between 2013 and 2025, to become by 2025 almost the same size as the economy of the United States.[13]

---

9 "China: The New Norm in Growth," Credit Suisse, September 28, 2012.

10 "China vs. 1970s Japan," Goldman Sachs, September 25, 2012.

11 Rahul Jacob, "China GDP: If Not 10% Then What?" *Financial Times* beyondbrics, December 6, 2012.

12 *Australia in the Asian Century White Paper: Australia's Roadmap for Navigating the Asian Century*, government of Australia, October 28, 2012.

13 "China 2025: A Clear Path to Prosperity," Jefferies Equity Research, January 1, 2013.

HOW FAST MUST CONSUMPTION GROW?

I find these 7 to 9 percent predictions implausible. They implicitly assume a surge in the growth rate of consumption that they never justify (except for the Jefferies research piece, which seems to argue that massive transfers from the state sector to the household sector along the lines I discussed in chapter 6 are easy to implement and highly likely to occur), and they deny, or at least fail to consider, that China's debt levels may be already too high.

But this implicit assumption about consumption growth is key. As everyone now recognizes, rebalancing in China requires that consumption grow significantly as a share of GDP over the next decade or more. China currently reports household consumption as representing about 35 percent of GDP. By how much would it have to rise for meaningful rebalancing to have occurred?

Globally, household consumption represents a fairly stable 65 percent of GDP. Over the past decade this average has encompassed a group of high-consuming countries, such as the United States and peripheral Europe, whose average consumption exceeded 70 percent, as well as a group of low-consuming countries, mainly in Asia, whose average consumption, excluding China, ranged from 50 to 58 percent.

It is unlikely that the high-consuming countries will be able to maintain their excess levels of consumption for the rest of this decade, and indeed their consumption rate has already come down substantially, with more to come. Peripheral Europe is in crisis, and the United States is taking steps to raise its savings rate. This means that low-consuming countries are also unlikely to be able to keep their consumption levels as low as they have in the past. A world with low-consuming countries requires high-consuming countries in order to balance.

If global consumption drops in the high consuming countries, with no corresponding rise in the low-consuming countries, it is unlikely that investment will rise quickly enough to replace it (why invest if no one is going to buy the output?), and so the global economy must respond with enough of a contraction in GDP to maintain consumption at roughly 60–65 percent. The great consumption and savings imbalances of the past that led to the current crisis, in other words, have to adjust. This means that if there are no longer large economies consuming 70 percent of more of their national income, the world is unlikely to be able to accommodate large economies consuming just 50–56 percent of their national incomes.[14]

Let us assume, nonetheless, that the world can accommodate a minimal amount of Chinese rebalancing. Within a decade Chinese household consumption, according to this assumption, will rise to no more than 50 percent of GDP, as difficult as it will be for the world to accept such low consumption from its second-largest economy.

How fast must Chinese consumption grow? To get household consumption to rise from 35 percent of GDP to 50 percent of GDP in a decade requires, it turns out, that household consumption growth outpace GDP growth by roughly 4 percentage points every year. This is just simple arithmetic, but it has important implications. It means that if we expect China to accomplish a minimal amount of rebalancing—one that will leave it with what will probably be the lowest consumption level by far for any major economy—predictions of 7–8 percent GDP growth rates implicitly involve predictions that consumption will grow over the next decade on average by 11–12 percent annually.

Clearly this isn't impossible, but is it plausible? In the past decade, under optimal conditions of explosive growth in investment, annual GDP growth of 10–11 percent, rapid growth in the global economy, and rapidly rising debt in China and abroad, consumption growth rates in China averaged 7–8 percent annually. But these optimistic economists are now projecting that as China's GDP growth slows sharply to 7–8 percent, as the global trade environment continues to deteriorate, and as China and the world are forced to come to grips with ballooning debt, household consumption will somehow surge to 11–12 percent annually. For this is what it means for China to rebalance while it is growing at 7–8 percent.

How can this surge in consumption growth happen? Technically there are only two ways, one or both of which must take place. First the household savings rate in China can collapse to 0 percent. Because the rich hold a disproportionate amount of China's savings, and since it is

---

14 See Michael Pettis, *The Great Rebalancing: Trade, Conflict, and the Perilous Road Ahead for the World Economy* (Princeton, N.J.: Princeton University Press, 2013).

very hard to drive down their savings rate, this would probably require in part a massive redistribution of wealth from rich to poor, but in any case it would also require a very unlikely surge in consumer credit. Given the weakness and inexperience of the retail credit market, this could happen, but it would be very worrisome because it would almost certainly lead to an explosion of bad debt.

The second way is for household income growth to outpace GDP growth—also by roughly 4 percentage points a year. One way of accomplishing this, as discussed in chapter 6, is to sharply raise wages, interest rates, and the value of the currency, although as we pointed out there are significant constraints in Beijing's ability to do so quickly enough. Another way to do so, again as we discussed in chapter 6, is to increase household wealth directly by massive transfers from the state sector; in this scenario, too, there are political constraints to doing so.

HOW QUICKLY CAN CHINA GROW?

I can see no other way logically of getting household consumption to rise quickly enough to accommodate both rebalancing and high GDP growth. Without a massive privatization program implemented quickly enough, in other words, I do not see how it is possible to get household consumption rates to soar enough to allow China to grow at 7–8 percent a year for the next decade (I exclude an explosion in consumer financing that brings the savings rate to zero as far too risky for the banking system and as extremely unlikely in a country with so weak a social safety net).

What I think more likely is that with the right policies Beijing might be able to maintain household income and consumption growth rates at the current level of 7–8 percent annually. This would not be easy and would involve moving fairly aggressively to raise wages and the interest rate, and a little less aggressively to raise the value of the currency. In addition, it would mean absorbing the resulting financial distress costs at first by allowing government debt to grow quickly and later by paying down this debt in the form of the sale of government assets.

Of course, investment growth rates would have to drop sharply, and maybe even contract. The more investment there is, the worse the debt imbalances become and the more costly the ultimate rebalancing. I believe Beijing understands this even if it will be unable to force powerful vested interests within the economy to understand this. In chapter 5 I showed that if we give China five years to bring investment down from its current level of 50 percent to 40 percent of GDP, which is the minimum suggested by the IMF study on Chinese overinvestment, Chinese investment must grow by roughly 4.5 percentage points or more below the GDP growth rate for this condition to be met.

The combination of steady growth in household income and consumption, and much lower investment growth, would bring average GDP growth rates over the next decade to between 3 and 4 percent. Over a decade, if this happens, China could accomplish the minimal amount of rebalancing required. Of course, this isn't the end of the story, because at 50 percent of GDP, Chinese household consumption would still be too low, and China would probably have to spend much of the 2020s also rebalancing. But at least it would represent sustainable growth.

What is more, it would be socially acceptable. As China shifts away from very inefficient capital-intensive growth powered by free money, the service and labor-intensive sectors would grow much more quickly, Chinese industries would become more efficient (and given the scale of the domestic economy, they would become globally competitive, too), and, most importantly, the household sector would continue to do as well, or nearly as well, as it has in the past two decades—household income would grow at rates that would be the envy of any country in the world even as China's GDP growth rates drop sharply.

Beijing has a difficult but urgent task, one that is likely to cause tremendous strains in the political system. Powerful sectors and families will resist or dilute any elimination of the distortions that have rewarded them so bountifully, but if these distortions are not eliminated, China's economy, like that of many fast-growing developing countries before it, will stall and its astonishing transformation will be a thing of the past.

These are the challenges the new leadership faces. Because the more successful Beijing is in managing the adjustment, the better for everyone—not just in China but also abroad. The United States and Europe should accommodate as much as possible a China that implements real structural reforms and rebalances its economy in a healthy way. Among other things, the world must tolerate some flexibility in the trade account for at least a few more years. The world should cooperate as much as possible with China's most difficult reform to date. It will not be easy.

I will finish this book with two recent notes, the first written by George Magnus, a senior adviser to UBS and one of the very few who consistently recognizes the global adjustments within which China must play an important role:

> In the wake of the 18th Congress of the Communist Party and the appointment of new leaders, this report considers why China has arrived at a point in its human and economic development where politics and the economy can't carry on as before.
>
> Far from being a Western rant, this view is common in China, not least among many top officials taking their positions in the new government, or previously in government. The country's biggest challenge is to manage economic rebalancing, which is about changing its growth model, which, in turn, requires major political reforms. With successful rebalancing, the slowdown in China need not be of great concern, except perhaps for the commodity sector, since the commodity-intensity of growth will fall sharply. Without it, the cyclical endgame for investment in the next 1–2 years could be highly disruptive.
>
> The consequences of rebalancing will not be trivial for China, or for the world economy. They will entail a significant slowdown in economic growth, with investment growing significantly slower, and consumption significantly faster, than GDP for many years. The consensus view is that this will get done in a new, 7.5–8.5 percent growth environment. This is an extremely unlikely outcome, and we wonder if the economic slowdown is only half over? Perhaps 5 percent is more likely. While half of China's growth in the last decade, this need be no disaster at all, but it depends on the management of rebalancing.
>
> For now, we can only speculate if new leaders will beat a path toward reform and rebalancing, or feel restrained because of opposition and pushback by vested interests. Internal "purity" reforms to the Party, further expansion of the income and social security system, and further incremental, financial sector reforms seem likely. But "implementation risk" figures prominently for many important political and economic reforms, which are less about box-ticking

and more a test of political will since they are of existential significance to the Party.

Beyond the politics, economic rebalancing is already leading to a slowdown in economic growth, which may have troughed momentarily. But as we explain, it is difficult for consumption to expand significantly more rapidly, while correcting the capital- and credit-intensity of GDP growth most likely means a sharp decline in investment growth.[15]

The second note is by Andy Xie, another of the few economists who recognized from the beginning the problems of China's unbalanced growth:

The past is over. But the future could be brighter if one recognizes reality. Raising productivity cannot be planned like building infrastructure. It happens as the market system optimizes the allocation of resources like capital and labor. Both are now beholden to the government. Hence, growth revival requires China to shift from the government to a market-led growth model. Reform, not more investment in the same stuff, is the key to reviving growth.[16]

---

15 "China: The End of Extrapolation," UBS, November 21, 2012.

16 Andy Xie, "Future Growth? The Answer Is Megacities," *Caixin*, December 6, 2012.

★

WHAT HAPPENS IF CHINA REVALUES THE RENMINBI?[1]

I t may help to understand how rebalancing works by examining what would happen to China if the central bank were to revalue the renminbi by some amount. Many people in China and abroad have argued that Beijing cannot afford to raise the value of the renminbi against the dollar because it would mean that China would take huge losses on its massive foreign exchange reserves. After all, if the renminbi rises by 10 percent against the dollar, with over $3 trillion in reserves the value of reserves will have necessarily declined by more than $300 billion in renminbi terms. So, the argument goes, raising the value of the renminbi would represent a loss of wealth for China.

This is almost completely wrong. China would not take losses anywhere close to that amount and may even take a gain if it revalues the currency. The mistaken perception has to do with misunderstanding the impact of changes in the value of a currency on the various relevant balance sheets.

First of all, will China as an economic entity lose if the renminbi is revalued by, say, 10 percent? Leaving aside the vigorous discussion about whether a renminbi revaluation would increase China's long-term growth prospects, the balance sheet impact of a revaluation depends on whether China is net long dollars or net short dollars. Because a revaluation is

---

1 Most of this appendix is based on my book *The Great Rebalancing: Trade, Conflict, and the Perilous Road Ahead for the World Economy* (Princeton, N.J.: Princeton University Press, 2012).

largely a balance sheet affair, this is the only relevant question in deciding what might be the immediate profit or loss impact of a revaluation of the renminbi.

There is no precise way of answering this question, because every economic entity in China implicitly has some complex exposure to the dollar (by which I mean foreign currencies generally) through current and future transactions. Generally speaking, however, China is likely to gain from a revaluation because after the revaluation it would be exchanging the stuff it makes for stuff it buys from abroad at a better ratio.

The value of what it sells abroad, in other words, will rise relative to the value of what it buys from abroad, and if we could correctly capitalize those values on the balance sheet, it would probably show that the Chinese balance sheet would improve with a revaluation of the renminbi. Some economists might make a more sophisticated argument that because China is a net creditor—that is, it is net long dollars—it would lose by a revaluation of the renminbi. This argument also turns out to be wrong, but for more complex reasons. To understand why, we need to consider the difference between a real loss and a realized loss.

If you believe that the renminbi is undervalued, then you must accept that China takes a "real" loss every time it exchanges a locally produced good or asset for a foreign one. After all, it is selling something for below its true value in exchange for something above its true value. It does not realize the loss, however, until it revalues the renminbi to its "correct" value. In other words, the People's Bank of China, as the representative of China's net creditor status, would immediately realize a loss when the renminbi revalues.

But this loss would not occur because of the revaluation. It occurred the very day the trade took place. When a Chinese producer sold goods to the United States and took payment in U.S. dollars, there was an unrealized economic loss equal to the undervaluation of the renminbi. This unrealized loss was passed on to the People's Bank of China when it bought the dollars from the exporter and paid renminbi. This loss, however, will not actually show up until the renminbi is revalued, which forces the real loss to be realized (which is to say, recognized as an accounting matter).

Postponing the revaluation, then, is not the way to avoid the loss—it is too late for that. The only way to avoid future additional loss is to stop making the exchange, which means, ironically, that the longer the People's Bank of China postpones the revaluation of the renminbi, the greater the real loss it will take because the more overvalued dollars it will have accumulated.

So a revaluation of the renminbi will not cause any real loss to China today. The loss has already occurred; it just hasn't been realized. But if the renminbi is revalued by 10 percent, the value of the People's Bank of China's assets would immediately decline by around $300 billion in renminbi terms. Because the Chinese measure their wealth in renminbi, isn't this a real additional loss for China?

No, it is not. All China or any other country can do with foreign exchange reserves is to pay for foreign imports or repay foreign obligations. Foreign reserves cannot be spent at home for obvious reasons, and so the real value of foreign reserves is the value of what it can do with the reserves abroad. But the value of things it can purchase or pay for abroad is unaffected by the exchange value of the currency. If the value of the reserves drops 10 percent in renminbi terms when the People's Bank of China revalues the renminbi, in other words, so does the value of all those foreign payments—by definition they must go down by exactly the same amount in renminbi terms.

This means that China as an economic entity takes no loss on the dollars it had in its foreign currency reserves. It can buy and pay for just as much "stuff" after the revaluation as it could before the revaluation—and, of course, the real value of money is what you can buy with it. So the real value of the reserves hasn't changed at all—just the accounting value in renminbi, but this simply recognizes losses that were already taken long ago when the trade was made and that should be a largely irrelevant number.

But that doesn't mean nothing at all happened. Although the Chinese overall balance sheet is probably a little better off with the revaluation, within China there are a whole set of winners and losers. Which is which depends on the structure of *individual* balance sheets. Basically everyone who is net long dollars against the renminbi loses in an appreciation, and everyone who is net short dollars against the renminbi wins.

In practice, this has important implications. Of course the People's Bank of China is a big loser. It has a hugely mismatched balance sheet in which it is long dollars against renminbi by around $3 trillion. Its balance sheet is mismatched because to fund the $3 trillion of dollar assets it has $3 trillion in renminbi liabilities (the People's Bank of China is actually probably insolvent).[2] As the dollar depreciates 10 percent against the renminbi, the value of the foreign exchange assets drops relative to renminbi by that amount, but of course the value of renminbi liabilities remains unchanged. The People's Bank of China, in other words, loses the renminbi equivalent of $300 billion of assets with no commensurate loss of liabilities, and so it takes a huge net loss.

There are other losers. Exporters and their employees, too, are naturally long dollars because of the nature of their business, and so they would lose from a revaluation. They are long dollars because more of the net value of their current and future production less current and future costs is denominated in dollars (they are "sticky" to dollar prices)—for example, labor costs, land, and almost all other inputs except imported components are valued in renminbi, while most revenue is valued in dollars.

So a revaluation of the renminbi would create a number of losers within China, most importantly the central bank, but if China as a whole takes no loss on the revaluation, then for every loser in China there must also be a winner. And who is it that wins? It turns out that nearly everyone else in China wins, because everyone in the country is implicitly short dollars to the extent that there are imported goods in his life.

The local tea seller is short dollars if his tea is delivered to him in gas-guzzling trucks, as is the family planning to visit Bali next year, as is the local provider of French perfumes, as is a teenager who wants to buy Nike shoes, and so pay for the corporate sponsorship of a Brazilian soccer star playing for a Spanish team. Every household and nearly every business in China is, in one way or another, an importer (and this is true in

2   This seemingly surprising statement is actually widely accepted by China-based economists. And why not? As of this writing the renminbi has revalued by roughly 30 percent since July 2005, which means that the value of its local currency liabilities has gone up by 30 percent relative to the value of its foreign currency assets.

every country), so unless these households own a lot of assets abroad they are effectively short dollars and will benefit from an appreciation in the renminbi.

As the renminbi revalues, the price of all of these imported goods and services automatically drops in renminbi terms, which means that households are able to purchase more goods and services for the same amount of money. The real value of their wealth and income rises by the change in the value of their expected imports.

Revaluing the renminbi, in other words, is important and significant because it represents a shift of wealth, largely from the People's Bank of China, exporters and wealthy Chinese residents who have stashed away a lot of their money in foreign banks, in favor of the rest of the country. Because much of this shift of wealth benefits households at the expense of the state and manufacturers, one of the automatic consequences of a revaluation would be an increase in household wealth and, with it, household consumption. Of course, if household consumption rises, then total savings will decline.

This is why revaluation is an important part of China's rebalancing strategy—it shifts income from the low-consuming state and wealthy individuals to higher consuming households, and so increases both household and national consumption. But there is more. As household consumption increases, the higher renminbi may reduce production in the tradable goods sector. The combination of higher consumption and lower production reduces the savings rate even more. If there is no change in investment, or if any reduction in investment is lower than the reduction in savings, China's trade surplus will automatically decline even further.

It is worth pointing out that the revaluation of the renminbi automatically shifted income within China and caused the savings rate to decline. For this to happen, it was wholly unnecessary that the Chinese reduced their fabled cultural propensity to save, or that the population aged, or that members of a younger, post–Cultural Revolution generation infused households with their spendthrift ways. Savings in China would automatically decline simply because the renminbi was revalued.

We can generalize from this example to consider that many kinds of wealth transfers within the country can have an impact on the trade balance—and this is the secret to understanding how policies affect the savings rate. Just as a revaluation of the renminbi implies a transfer of wealth from the People's Bank of China to Chinese households, and so is likely to increase consumption, other transfers from the state sector to households can have the same effect.

INDEX

ABOUT THE AUTHOR

Michael Pettis is a Beijing-based senior associate in the Carnegie Asia Program. An expert on China's economy, Pettis is a professor of finance at Peking University's Guanghua School of Management, where he specializes in Chinese financial markets.

From 2002 to 2004, he also taught at Tsinghua University's School of Economics and Management and, from 1992 to 2001, at Columbia University's Graduate School of Business. He is a member of the Institute of Latin American Studies Advisory Board at Columbia University as well as the Dean's Advisory Board at the School of Public and International Affairs.

Pettis worked on Wall Street in trading, capital markets, and corporate finance since 1987, when he joined the sovereign debt trading team at Manufacturers Hanover (now JPMorgan). Most recently, from 1996 to 2001, Pettis worked at Bear Stearns, where he was managing director principal heading the Latin American capital markets and the liability management groups. He has also worked as a partner in a merchant-banking boutique that specialized in securitizing Latin American assets and at Credit Suisse First Boston, where he headed the emerging markets trading team.

In addition to trading and capital markets, Pettis has been involved in sovereign advisory work, including for the Mexican government on the privatization of its banking system, the Republic of Macedonia on the restructuring of its international bank debt, and the South Korean Ministry of Finance on the restructuring of the country's commercial bank debt.

He formerly served as a member of the Board of Directors of ABC-CA Fund Management Company, a Sino-French joint venture based in Shanghai. He is the author of several books, including *The Great Rebalancing: Trade, Conflict, and the Perilous Road Ahead for the World Economy* (Princeton University Press, 2013).

CARNEGIE ENDOWMENT
FOR INTERNATIONAL PEACE

The Carnegie Endowment for International Peace is the oldest international affairs think tank in the United States. Founded in 1910, it is known for excellence in scholarship, responsiveness to changing global circumstances, and a commitment to concrete improvements in public policy.

Carnegie launched a revolutionary plan in 2006 to build the first global think tank and since then has transformed an American institution into one fitted to the challenges of a globalized world. Today, Carnegie has research centers in Beijing, Beirut, Brussels, Moscow, and Washington as well as a program in Almaty.